Vanishing Acts

Vanishing Acts

MS | Mill Street Press. Martha's Vineyard. *an imprint of Parkway Press.*

Helen Ashmore

Cataloging information:

Ashmore, Helen Virginia Shinkle

Vanishing Acts: an odyssey. Mill Street Press.
an imprint of Parkway Press, Ltd. West Tisbury MA 02575

1. Travelers, American 2.American miscellany 3. Biographies, women
   I.Title 1989   920   818   920.72

First edition 1989
L.C.#88-62523   ISBN:938270-04-4

Simultaneous paperback first edition: LC#88-62523   ISBN:938270-05-2

Manufactured in the United States of America

10 9 8 7 6 5 4 3 2 1

Also by Helen Ashmore:

Lady Chesterfield's Stepdaughter: Poems

Musicals with Mike White:

Home
Give the World Your Dream

Book design: Milstein + Ashmore
Cover sculpture: Barcelona artist (unknown)
Cover photo: Betsy Corsiglia
Author photo: William Lafferty
Design consultants: Kolodny & Rentschler
Typeface: Palatino 10 point roman

I would like to express my gratitude to those who have helped me by reading and making valuable suggestions for the taming of myriad unruly versions of this manuscript: Emily Mehling and Richard Woodward early on, Suzanne Matson from the first draft to the last. I thank Anne Robin Ashmore for bringing some impetuous transcriptions of French into obedient good form, and Tony Rezendes of the West Tisbury post office for meeting innumerable arcane requests with alacrity and enduring good nature. I hereby thank as well some disembodied voices at the New York Public Library telephone reference service for patient and kindly clarification of numerous popular culture facts.

I thank with the thanks there are no words for both Margaret Barnes and Ann Fielder of the West Tisbury Public Library who have for years provided unflagging friendship, encouragement, support and joy.

Finally, I am grateful to my publisher Sam Milstein for his tenacious faith in me and in this project--now, because of his inexhaustible enthusiasm, this book. Working together with total control over every aspect of this project has been a rare publishing privilege and challenge.

Flannery O'Connor said of some editors with which she was afflicted early in her career that she could not look forward with composure to a lifetime of working with people like that, whose objections seemed to her connected with her work's *virtues*. Sam's enthusiasm seems to me always to be for what virtues I may have as a writer.

For fragments blatantly committed, for non-words obstinately asserted, for quotation marks incorrigibly avoided and commas stingily underused--for these and all other crimes against convention, I shoulder full responsibility, gesturing, however, with slight cowardice and pretension, perhaps, toward courageous precedents long since set by Joyce and Beckett.

Helen Ashmore
November 3, 1988
West Tisbury, Martha's Vineyard

For Jack

The year has come, the one we all look forward to, believing it will never come. But this is it. I look at my children, tan and strong and beautiful as they laugh and talk with friends at the dining room table, and I think 'I have been used. The fates have used me to produce this superior race of beings, and now they are through with me.'

Robin and Joel, who do not know that they are higher forms of life or that I am obsolete, see me looking at them and ask what's for dessert.

Ducunt fata volentem, nolentem trahunt says the philosopher Seneca. 'The fates guide him who will; him who won't they drag.' I am grateful for the guidance and the dragging too.

We all get notions. The fates generously corrected my benighted one that I did not want children. When our first child was born, I looked at my watch, although I did not wear a watch, and said, 'Well, Jack, it looks like we're in for twenty years.' The fates dragged me through eight years of marriage--to a man I love. But I took with a will to the complex gift of children.

Still, there has been this tugging at my heart--there is a world out there!--a restlessness in me all these years. I have been such a homebody that I've thrown myself onto the front lawn, returning from a long vacation, and said 'I'll never leave you again,' then left again again.

But we have done all we can do for one another just now, these children, this old house and I. The time has come. The children are grown. The house is sold. And I am leaving home, going to see what's out there in the world that I've so longed for.

What follows is testimony to the world I found or that found me when I threw myself into it, a person without place. I lived in a kind of ecstacy for years, without appointed rounds or required responses. And where, as Cyril Connolly says, there is no appointment there can be no disappointment. Once I stepped out of my role as mother in that long-run show, I was freed of two forms of appointment: other people's expectations of my behavior, and my expectations that the world should behave in a certain way toward me. I was free in a world entirely brave and new. I loved it, feared it, laughed to see it and wanted, often, to bear witness to it.

It was the evanescent quality of this life, of these events that attracted me, always. Anything that smacked of life as plot, with incidents marching triumphantly, inexorably to love and marriage, power and money--*all that*--was assigned to oblivion. So, for every incident reported here, there are many left untold, of relations that would be considered normal and on-track and therefore important by most readers. But it was precisely this sort of *achieved*, 'well here we are' life that did not interest me, and its devaluation in these pages is as it should be.

I hold with Aristotle that nature is not being but becoming. In my experience, to be fully alive is to be alone, suspended in events without a future or a past and over which one has no illusion of control. It would be dreaming to think that life can always be so, but it is pure gift and privilege to have had it that way for a time.

A last issue, genre. When people say, 'why don't you make this a novel?' the answer is, a book of poems or photos maybe--a novel, *never*. Even if I could write one which I couldn't. Some names are changed to protect some egos; that is the only deliberate fiction in this work.

The characters of Milan Kundera's novel, *The Book of Laughter and Forgetting* provide the last word here.

--Novels are the fruit of the human illusion that we can understand our fellow man. But what do we know about each other?

--Nothing....

--The only thing we can do...is to give an account of our own selves. Anything else is an abuse of power. Anything else is a lie.

Vanishing Acts

an odyssey

Helen Ashmore

Prologue

*He found in the world without as actual
what was in his world within as possible.*

Ulysses, James Joyce

ree at last

on the road and sailing down the old Santa Fe trail, we're going for trail's end at cop-taunting speed. Susan, dear long-time friend in art appreciation and other crimes, takes the wheel and the responsibility for speeding while I hang out the window rhapsodizing over the haybales that flash by.

We have left Kansas City at midday to do most of the trip at night, and we eat up almost two-hundred miles of gray-green Kansas summer in three hours, mindful of the pioneers who rocked and rattled for a week to cover this same distance in their wagons, throwing out the ornate armoires as their choices narrowed.

Then it is dusk settling over a hill that rises beyond Salina in a glowing haze of golden dust. Then quiet. Easing into the night, soft we go by soft summer sounds: the voices of children on bicycles calling each others' names like bells, the chorus of cicadas crackling like electric wires, the soft hum of our tires on the highway going through the small Kansas towns this summer night like a passing thought.

Near dawn we stop to rest, nestling our heads into our jackets, birds head-under-wing. A weird, plaintive two-note cry disturbs the quiet. The cock? Where then is the doodle-do? A peacock? The cry repeats, mysterious and clear. Then the unmistakable attack bark of a Doberman in a sunrise frenzy behind a fence nearby, discovering us.

Semis roar by in a spare caravan, doing the Doppler effect. One increases in volume, roars violently by, then fades into its future leaving behind a lacuna of white silence before another roar begins to gather toward us.

Visions of the haybales we have seen today in their varied forms play across my fading consciousness. They first appeared as haybales doing what haybales do. They stood there, golden spikey boxes, neatly waiting, minding their business along the fences. Or they were wedged so tightly into a big, open-sided shed that it seemed their farmer was rich in hay and that his cows would have their fill all the bleak plains winter long--if only he could solve the Chinese puzzle: how to get the first bale out.

Then the haybales started to show character, suggesting by their attitudes and poses that like all things in nature they were not being but becoming.

There were ambitious, progress-minded bales that escaped the barns and fence rows to stand upon each others' shoulders by the road, creating a city of tall, imposing buildings. They towered over the prairie and the speeding cars as if to say, 'Look here, boys. We're the business of the land out here, and big business too.'

Maverick hayrolls crowded along the railroad tracks drawn by the excitement--the promise of another life!--waiting to jump boxcars and get out. And while they waited, they could eavesdrop on the conversations buzzing through the wires above, the words of worlds beyond the farm.

Young and playful hayrolls would hear us coming and strike statue poses in the middle of a game of rolling down the path their farmer had cut of and for them in a gentle slope of the green Flint Hills.

Haystack mammoths lined up outside a tiny white-spired church, waiting to go in and sing the anthems, put quarters in the plate.

Haystacks like loaves for giants waited resolutely for the first slice of the big knife across their backs.

Hayrolls slightly melted down by rain stood companionably about in a pink sunset on a golden evening field beneath the mountains of New Mexico--a short, shaggy herd of radiant, mythic sheep grazing at day's end.

Here and there an old-timer haystack, a haystack like a stack of hay, a monument to the simpler past, stood wondering what the variety and fuss was all about.

Love, says Ortega, is what gets your attention. And so, perhaps I am in love with haybales. Susan, true fellow traveler, listens to my passion as a girlfriend does, allowing me my rapture and hoping I will get over it soon. I don't. I am still in love with haybales. And the road.

Sightseeing, soundhearing, the trip to Taos becomes in memory chiefly sounds: the sound of our own voices as we sing our way across the widening vistas of the blue western highway in a black car like a quarter note in the landscape--*I'll be down to get you in a taxi honey, better be ready 'bout half past eight'* drifting in our wake over the mountaintops.

The deep voice of the big, dark-eyed man at the last truck stop in Kansas, who crossed his huge arms at me and said 'what's the trouble?' in such a tone and with such a look that I was followed halfway across starlit Colorado with the feeling that he knew the trouble was not the water pump. It was women like us, women who had no man like him. Right, right. One like that, please, a man from my midwestern, country-town adolescence, the men time does not touch. Like earth, like rock. Would I remember how to talk to a man like that? Of course I would. But talk was not the issue here. And still his voice will echo, and I know that years from now I will remember him as though he were standing before me.

More sounds. The palpable quiet of Canyon Road broken by the footfalls of Bob and Susan and Ken and me on the trail of the good life in Santa Fe, that town of sunny, average art and exceptional cooking. The gentle creak of the giant hammock in creaking cottonwoods in moonlight.

The racking rattle of the car door as we clambered up the dirt road to Gail's bed and breakfast house that clings to the mountainside in the prodigious bowl of sky above Arroyo Hondo. The eerie train-whistling geese. The yapping dogs that came wagging at us rough and tumble when we achieved their hilltop home.

The rustle of the cottonwoods again when storm clouds rose and rolled around the 360-degree horizon, the gods' great inverted bowl of sky that we sat on a rim of, on Gail's roof at sundown, drinking wine and saying 'ah the world, ah life.'

The tom-toms at midnight, bumping beneath the high, frail, whining pipe, the music growing closer, closer still until we knew the tribe had seen the women and were coming for us, and we collapsed in giggles. The music grown full-bodied right outside our window now, with singing and whomping and something like a tuba joining in. Gail, called for help, explaining that the My Foundation on the adjoining hill was celebrating a composer's latest work, that the mountains made the sounds do these eerie visitations.

Gail's Indian companion Jerry splashing in the bathtub by our room, singing Indian lore; then in the morning whistling the same melodies as he worked around the yard--a variation on 'Whistle While You Work' that made us laugh with joy at the paradox. The clattering of the knives and forks on plates against our awed silence at breakfast the morning he came back from a Wyoming pilgrimage and sat there shirtless, two holes like stigmata torn in his chest by tribal rite.

The quiet of the early morning broken by greetings from the goslings and the dogs and the My people at it again already, their music piping thinly in thin air as they walked slowly in a circle back and forth, then one-two-three kicked back then forward, stopped, received the pipe of offering just as the earth rolled over and--pop!--the sun was on.

The whir of bike wheels up the mountain highway where Susan stopped to ask directions and was taken in by Christian Indians to use the phone, perhaps to be convert-ed, leaving me high and still in brilliant air, ecstatic pagan pilgrim in the driveway.

...

At the Taos World Championship Heavyweight Poetry Contest we bore witness one night to a spirit foreign to readings as we had known them: generosity, wild variety, and appreciative fun. The poems were intelligible, the poets' voices clear. Their leader, Peter Rabbit, affirmed his guruship with the recurrent Vedic incantation: 'Mr. Rabbit is here with the shit.' And the games were on.

David, an Indian, read an Indian poem about the power of nature. Mary Ann read to a dead friend, Tommy.

An Indian woman got up, reeled off a short intense poem about a short intense storm, and sat down.

Tracy recited what he called 'a former epic, now four lines' about polar bears invading the streets of an Alaskan frontier town. A young woman who had never read before stood up, pretty, frail, determined, and read beginner's work.

Bill Gersh, painter, read the work of others: of mad Jack Micheline's fifties funny stuff, then of the impassioned Zinn, a Taos friend of Gersh now, like Tommy, dead.

A man in a wheelchair read poems approving darkness, large women and rhymes, a large, dark woman attentive at his side and certain as an end rhyme.

Wherefore this genial enclave in a world of petty poet politics, we wondered. 'This is not the way they do it in Kansas City,' we said to one another as laughter rose from the café courtyard into the mountain summer night all stars.

Where was the male madness of the West? The killer competition, swaggering bravado? It was not there, though Dennis Hopper was, famous at just that time for only one thing--rashness. But he bounced, small and intense and cordial, off a few poet friends and disappeared.

Gersh, noting Susan's dark beauty with an enthusiasm that bordered on persistence, invited us along to the poets' hangout, a big bar nearby where a band was playing in this same ample spirit. Everyone got into the act and everyone was having a good time, passing around the limelight in boozy camaraderie. By one o'clock half the customers were on the stage. A big blonde gave us 'It Might As Well Be Spring' in Chris Connor's voice. Then a sturdy man in bottle glasses and in Billy Eckstine's voice did Hey There.

It is an evening I pull out in memory from time to time when caught in others not like it at all.

Arriving home in Kansas where the boxes are stacked high around the barren room, I find Joel sitting in the living room in one of the huge straight-backed oak chairs we call the bishops' chairs. He looks like he might, in the manner of Miss Havisham in *Great Expectations*, make a career out of being abandoned.

--Are you o.k?

--Yeah, I'm o.k.

--Forgive me if I say you do not look so good.

--I'm tired.

--You look exhausted.

--Yeah. I'm tired.

--Well, uh...did you have fun?

--Not exactly.

--Too much freedom?

--Something like that.

--License. Too much license. You hungry?

--Starving.

Then Joel gets up, walks to the kitchen and beckons for me.

--Well? he says.

--Well what?

--Well, here we are. We've got a mom. We've got a kitchen. We've got a starving boy. *Well?*

And so I make a last meal in the home we just about no longer have. The next day Joel goes back to the university and the day after, the movers come. The last night there, I'm sleeping on the floor at midnight when I hear a knock. It's Joel and a friend.

--Oh, Joel. You'll have to sleep on the floor. This show is shut down, over.

Joel doesn't quite believe it. The mom is out of service. The mom's as good as gone. The mom at just that moment feels like a perfect creep.

...

Eastward ho, Aunt Helen riding shotgun. We are on our way to Martha's Vineyard island where Ernest and Ann Manheim have offered us their island home for Indian Summer. This Kansas City connection on the Vineyard goes back to the fifties when Rita and Thomas Hart Benton were spending summers on the Vineyard and lured along Kansas City University friends with them. It was Rita Benton who found the Manheims the house Aunt and I are headed for now.

It is the last day of August. The landscape should be parched in the central plains. But north on highway 35 from Kansas City and east on old highway 36 we find the rolling countryside richly turned out in lovely dull greens and blues and a hundred shades of yellow going brown: Kansas artist Robert Sudlow's colors, flicked with blessings of light.

Celebrating entry into Illinois, we stop at a big tented fruit stand where the flies are clearly in control of the situation. I pick out one lonely peach and present myself to a large doughy woman with a tall, dark imposing beehive hairdo, now a flyhive. She looks at my puny peach and then me, and she refuses to take my money.

--You may as well just eat it, she says with unfettered disgust, like those snarling waitresses who order you into your booth with a ferocious, 'Enjoy your meal!'

At dusk we cross the Wabash and roll into Rockville, Indiana (pop. 2785) through ranks of stately spruces and a scatter of covered bridges that dot the landscape like haybales. We are in covered-bridge country where a festival is held in honor of the thirty-eight local ones each October.

I eat my peach while Aunt gets ready for dinner, and the flyhive lady's anger revisits me. Now I am sorry I was so faint-hearted; it is ambrosial, a peach among peaches.

Rockville is Our Town, with a large clock-tower bell ringing in the hours on the town square. Some teenagers sit on the curb at one corner of the square, kicking at rocks and gossiping quietly, 'Well, I don't see why she didn't just tell me...' while, down at the Short Stop restaurant, their more manic peers rollick around pool tables and the parking lot, and their elders--broad, placid couples wearing plaids and polyester--chew fried chicken in the plastic booths next door.

The romance of the small highway gives way to the hard, jerky reality of getting around Indianapolis and Fort Wayne, and we are glad, turning down a quiet street in Farmington, Michigan the next evening, to find Uncle and Ellie in their flowering yard. We spend the evening looking at slides from the old days when we spent long summer vacations at Uncle's cottage on the lake. 'The lake' in our family means Runyan Lake in Fenton, Michigan, although one says there are other lakes. 'The lake' to me signals Eden; no innocence or joy seems whole save those tan hours with my sister in the sun. I spend my dreams with her in sailboats and on skis.

The next morning we take big highway 94 to Port Huron, trying to escape the American Labor Day weekend traffic. Instead we are trapped in the thick of it: the biggest vacation jam in North America features us at its center, in the middle of the Niagara Falls-U.S.A. bridge for an hour before we make our break.

The Canadian highway numbering system, the principle of which seems to be to change numbers as often and as arbitrarily as possible (that is, whether the road changes course or not), makes us dive for the fatherland.

Down highway 20 and into the Finger Lake country of upstate New York, we reach Geneva where we find what may be the saddest surviving specimen of the old individual cabin motel.

Although the man who rents us our Tobacco Road shack has owned the Blue Spruce for only thirty years, it has clearly been on the decline that brought it to its present dilapidation much longer. But we are glad to find anything in the middle of this glut of tourists.

In the morning out front like large dark squashes that have sprung up overnight in an invasion worthy of the body snatchers, a crop of battered junk heaps announce by proclamations boldly spray-painted on their trunks that they are champions, prize winners at local races: this warrior Chevy in '82, that battleship Dodge in '80.

We stop at Patsy's cafe where the good old boys hang out. They wear no feed caps, a phenomenon we have never seen. Midwestern country boys wear feed caps at their hangouts. It is required, Aunt Helen says.

A young woman enters, agitated, to complain at length to a man twenty years her senior that no one has picked her up when she tried to hitchhike over.

--People know me. I'm from the country, she says, emphasizing each word.

Her voice gets louder and louder as she recites her anger. She is so angry that no one has picked her up that soon she is shouting at the man who sits there, quiet, eating eggs. (Her brother, father, lover?) They have just left her standing there in the early morning upstate New York fog where *they all know her, they even know her coat.*

Cars are stopped beside the heavily fogged road, but we creep on in our own fog, and manage to go shopping. Aunt Helen always knows these things: the local lore and products. In Herkimer county, it's the cheese. In Cazenovia we discover the local wine at Planes Cayuga Vineyard. We buy a 'Chancellor Red' named after Bob Planes, proprietor and, incidentally, chancellor of the local college. Cortland apples, maple syrup and maple candy from a roadside stand in West Winfield complete our upstate spree.

Waiting on the entrance ramp to 90 for an hour outside Albany, we chomp on cheese and apples. Soon we are well into Massachusetts. Feeling smug after our Kentucky Fried at Palmer, we head for the back highways again, and they prove charming for some minutes. Then it is a hair-raising dodge from 32 to 74 to 44 to 101. I chant it like a mantra trying to remember what it is I'm trying to do, through thick traffic on dark and unfamiliar, narrow two-lane roads all wild with eager-to-get-home vacationers passing us blind on hills. State lines flash by so often, we don't even try to keep track of what state we're in.

We're glad to be alive in any state at all by the time we get to Providence. Exhausted by the real America, we take coldhearted, eight-lane 195 that gets us to New Bedford double quick. Up winding 28 through the ugly terrors of Buzzards' Bay commercial strip and traffic dervishes, and down the last few quiet miles to Woods Hole, we just make the last ferry of the night.

We cross the six miles of Atlantic ocean under a fearful, black sky and drive off the ferry into the island jumble in a dream. A sign that says West Tisbury leads us up a road of magic in the summer midnight. We move through a wonderland of dark, curving tunnels lined with a profusion of leaves. A thousand oak arms reach over us in benediction. We are safe, arrived.

...

Vanishing Acts

an odyssey

Ever since Joyce...we have been aware of the fact that the greatest adventure in our lives is the absence of adventure.

The Book of Laughter and Forgetting, Milan Kundera

*T*here is the sea

of course, but even more than that this island in September is its light. The luminescence of the gray-green twisted oaks on curving up-island roads in fall is a shining so transcendent that it seems a spiritual rather than a mere physical light. An explosion of metaphysical 'message' hits me every time I turn certain corners like the one on Music Street where, on a bank of pale blonde grasses spiked with wine-dark sheaves, serpentine oak branches reach out for passersby.

Enchanted is the word, and I would not like to count the times during the first weeks here I found myself headed off the road into a ditch or a charming rough stone wall. I am better now and can keep my car on the road, but I am never unaware of this entrancing light.

And I am not even counting the brilliant pink and purple sunsets on the beaches. I know now to pull off and stop when the sky begins to gather all the colors, pale and soft, beyond the muted radiance of the globe lamplights along the Oak Bluffs ocean drive--globes like so many small, full moons coaxed into earthly service high on pedestals, but not so high as once they were.

On the first day of fall, a Saturday, the weather is perfect on the island. Everybody is out. Along the beach road there are fishers, bikers, kiters, joggers, wind-surfers, swimmers, sailors--all out in force enjoying this sunny day.

Down the beach away from the crowds, a very young couple--she a pretty boy-like girl, slim and small, he a handsome girl-like boy, soft-featured and supple--play and laugh, happy in love. It rings out in their voices, echoes in their walks. They go to sit on a rock together where he tries to hug her into his Adam's side, to take Eve back. She wraps herself into him and they kiss.

A few yards away from them, a potato sack of a man, a man no longer young, has thrown himself out on the sand in his bluejeans to air his large white stomach. He touches it occasionally as though to say someone should. Then he brushes the sand from his cheek ever ever so gently, as if he knows that love is where you find it.

...

3

West Tisbury is a tiny country village where horses chomp in the barnyards and haybales melt in the fields, where mallards and swans glide mellow on the Old Mill Pond. It is a usual New England village in every respect except one. It is at sea. Six miles off the Cape Cod coast, it is the up-island heart of Martha's Vineyard.

The town consists principally of Alley's General Store and Post Office on the main road. Beyond Alley's parking lot and laundromat is Paul's house, then the white-spired, white picket-fenced Greek Revival Congregational church, both facing the main road. Across Music Street, which borders the church on the west, stands the tall gray mansard-roofed town hall--well, taller than the thirty feet now allowed by building code--with the rambling Grange across a field from it. The tiny Free Public Library is nestled in behind them a short way down Music Street. And that is about it for the town center.

Down by the Old Mill Pond is the Police Office, formerly the one room school, then the town hall. Tall, uniformed policemen feed the ducks and swans and geese each day, an official law-enforcement duty, and one that at eventide shows greater grace than most. It is a droll, endearing sight to see big George Manter with fifteen fat ducks waddling purposefully behind him, after, for all they know, their ma.

The police office is an unassuming, homey house, festive with daffodils and forsythia in spring, cozy in autumn's golden grasses. Like the town it protects, it seems to have a steady rhythm, a kind of sanity and natural good. I say this. The tourists who are waved down in front of it and handed fifty dollar fines for speeding through the duck crossing may see it in another light.

Alley's, 'Dealers in Almost Everything,' is a double-gabled, shingled building that looks like what it is: the General Store and Post Office. The masculine center of West Tisbury, its regulars are carpenters and correspondents, celebrities and other ordinary citizens whose pickups

4

and vans fill the parking lot and line the road along the long front porch, a Labrador retriever presiding over every steering wheel.

The personable, gray-bearded man who owns the store and makes the coffee here is Charlie Parton, distinguished pediatric surgeon who has served in the Peace Corps and is now in an incarnation as storekeeper. Tina his wife works by his side or nearby in the office tallying.

The property is still owned by Alleys, the third family of owners in one hundred and twenty-five years. And Alley's still has an Alley in the person of postmaster James, who dominates a tiny postal kingdom at the back of the store. A ruddy, rough-handed man with an amused demeanor, a brusque, gallant manner and ex-wives enough--one local gossip says--to start a basketball team, Jim hands out quips and compliments with his neighbors' daily mail. From the sound of things, the window where he presides most mornings, succeeded by Tony Rezendes in the afternoons, is where all the news in town breaks first and all important business and political exchanges take place.

Jim's sure he doesn't know why anyone would think they need more of address than a person's name and West Tisbury MA 02575.

--Do they think I can't find my own people at my own post office? he says.

When Jim leaves work, getting into his Bronco with his big flat-brimmed hat on, he looks more like a Wyoming rancher than a New England postmaster. He emanates a spirit of the town, a kind of paradoxical, pioneer, big-country freedom that is hard to find in mainland America. ('America over there,' local citizens say, especially when they're disgusted by what's going on politically: by Meese's being made attorney general, say.)

For newcomers in town, Jim and Tony act with nearly inexhaustible patience and good will as information, please.

5

When Aunt Helen wants to visit Vincent Beach at Chilmark where she has gone long ago with Rita Benton and Ann Manheim, it is Tony who fields my question.

--That's a uh, that's a...nude beach, he says.

--I know, Aunt Helen says, brisk and game beside me in her more than eighty years.

--You go past the cemetery and when you see the airplane propeller on the right, look for a dirt road to the left right there and take it.

With few exceptions, the good swimming beaches on the island are private and cannot be found without this kind of inside information. By a law enacted in the 1640's, the public cannot walk above the low tide mark on private beaches anyway, which sounds like an invitation to some very wet not to say dangerous walking. That law is being challenged now.

Meanwhile, most beach roads are not marked on maps, except enough to send you into a maze of bumpy, sandy lanes leading into one another endlessly. Maps stimulate blood pressure and shock absorber sales. They do not get the novice to the beach.

One feels that this is no accident. And I would like to know how many weekend or day-trip tourists full of zest have come to stretch out on the beaches and spent the day instead lost in the sandy maze of back roads, rocking and roiling like ships in a storm on the high seas, before missing the last ferry to the mainland and spending the night in their cars on standby for passage home.

Down a small, dirt road off Music Street, the tradition of keeping tourists at arm's length is witnessed by a totem arrangement of signs that announce: Doyle, Hodgson, Burt, and Wrong Road. On Middle Road, a beautifully worn old green gate requests No Trespassing, PLEASE. Better yet, says Polly on the porch one day, was the sign on Middle

Road--alas no longer there--that requested, Harmless Trespassers Only.

...

Off-season the hands-down major event of any day in West Tisbury is the drive up to Alley's to get the mail. I don't want to say that it makes you feel smug to make this modest trip. But it makes you feel awfully good. You ease past the Mill Pond with a great deal of satisfaction in its grace and serenity. You pass the tiny traffic island with the oak trees stretching in the sun. And you arrive alongside the board porch of Alley's, like a boat mooring at a pier. Here it is: this place, these people. Nothing about the feel and creak of the board porch under your feet disrupts the glow of bonhomie about you now. And by the time you open the green door into the sights and smells of a whole world of good made manifest in glorious simplicity before you, you think, where else would anybody want to be but here?

You get your mail and go over the major issues of the day in brief with Jim or Tony. Behind you stands an insistently disheveled woman in jeans and sweater and the island trance. She is talking half to herself, half to Tony as you wander off smiling at your mail. On the porch, among the carpenters who aren't so distracted as most other citizens, you sit in the fall sun on the edge of the porch, leaning on a post and conversing with your mail.

Then you go back in to the ice-cream freezer cum newspaper stand and choose the world you wish to be a citizen of today: Boston with the *Boston Globe*, the voice of the biggest small town in the world; New York with the *Times* and all the world that's fit to print; Cape Cod with their *Times*; or the island with its upstart *Vineyard Times* or venerable *Gazette*.

Without a challenge, the big newspaper day is Friday when the *Vineyard Gazette* comes out. No one on the island doesn't read the *Gazette*. A community newspaper in a unique sense, it reports the local news giving about equal column inches to four-legged, two-legged (feathered and featherless) and six-finned inhabitants. The paper was made famous by Henry Beetle Hough whose country-editor musings have aroused the affections of people all over this overstressed planet. (They have provoked their share of ire as well among tougher-minded citizens, who can find them cloying.) Hough has made a long career of advising the people about what is important in this life and what is not. An example of this value system: the *Gazette* runs a banner line of poetry above every issue's masthead. Big.

At a counter spilling over with vegetables from town clerk Heidi Schultz's garden, you get a Charlie-made cup of coffee, strong, perfect, fifty cents the cup. Nowhere will you find a stouter cup of true Columbian. And every day there is a lovely, rich and steaming soup for lunch: acorn squash, vegetarian chili, sweet potato curry, fresh creamed parsnip chowder. Diane's soups--Diane is a pretty, pleasant young woman, prematurely graying from her French res- taurant training perhaps--are the island's answer to home, mother and trace minerals. The creations in her cauldron are not standard workman's fare. As Diane is no ordinary cook, these are no ordinary workmen.

Just listen to them. With soup or coffee and newspaper, you go back out again, this time to sit on the edge of the porch or in one of the two beat-up plastic web lawn chairs--although these are preferred, usually, by tourists and by residents under sixteen years of age--to read and to catch the carpenters in action.

The island carpenters and builders, a breed of Titans tromping by in heavy boots, levis, plaid shirts and down vests, are the soul of West Tisbury. Their conversations exude skill and intelligence, transforming Alley's porch at coffee time into a sort of combined workshop and think tank. Many of the younger ones are college educated, and it is not at all unusual to find yourself in conversation with a man who makes his living as a carpenter while enjoying the personal advantage of a PhD in philosophy or literature.

8

One poet-carpenter is busy writing haiku poems on the backs of the staircase risers he is building.

--But who will ever see them? someone asks.

He replies with sureness and anticipation, joy.

--Some other crew. Some other guys like us, he says. They'll see them. Houses go up by human hands, houses like this one. Someone will be working in here again a hundred years or so from now.

Dr. John Scott who has a PhD in architecture is restoring one of the island's oldest houses. He is finding just such evidence of human hands. The work, he says, is both rewarding and depressing. Depressing because the seasons of three hundred years have done a lot of damage to the house, and rewarding because working through the layers of the years, scraping with patience to the house's origins, he has found a wall 'the color of the island--not gray or blue or green, but a smoky green-blue-gray,' and he has matched the color for repainting the interior.

On another wall, another buried treasure: the faded, loving drawings of a boy, he thinks, of old square-rigger ships, a kind that in the old days would have come here.

One wall is daub and wattle, 'a process that disappeared from England in 1670 or so,' says Dr. Scott, although no one will ever call him that on Alley's porch. He is and has been, will be to his neighbors always, John.

A favorite island thing to say is that everyone on the island is retired. Another is that every builder is the best builder on the island. John Early, a West Tisbury builder with a best reputation, builds houses people fork over monstrous sums for: one, two, three million dollars not uncommonly. Early is a town selectman, regarded in all he does as able and intelligent. His crew tears around the island in white trucks because, John says, they are the good guys.

The credentials of such a crew as his were perhaps best stated by an old-timer who watched them work for quite a while one day without a word in good New England fashion. But as he left, he called out his admiration.

--Watching you boys work is a real pleasure. Compared to other crews I've seen around here lately, it's like watching the Celtics after watching some JV team.

Even off season there may be a pair of tourists at Alleys, somewhat displaced and immediately identifiable. There they are among the levis in their spanking new resort attire: the woman in a hairdo and full makeup, the man in jaunty colors like a flag lost from the golf course. They reel off the porch in a daze after paying island prices for their Kodachrome, get into their rental Escort, and creep up State Road. The wife bends over an island map and points this way, then that. The husband brings the car to a decisive halt by the Town Hall.

Sometimes you just sit in your car in the parking lot for a while, reading the mail again and watching with absent minded pleasure as some old timer pulls his pickup slowly out onto the road and eases away into another day. There is something very reassuring about these old New England men; their solid visages like cliff sides, their simple style of going in the world, affirm a world in order, one that stays in place--a world in short the way the world should be.

...

Down Music Street--so called because a number of families in the early days had pianos that would set the street ringing with music on summer nights--sits the small, welcoming West Tisbury Free Public Library. A white, two-story, wooden Victorian doll house with deep-gabled windows in a mansard roof, it is nestled in cozy among oaks and bayberry, bittersweet and ivy. Kaleidoscope lights and shadows play on the leaf-strewn walk and across the

10

facade. An oak-shaded bench beckons by the side door. The 'closed' sign dangles like an invitation to come in.

The tall downstairs room is a friendly maze of small bulging shelves topped with oversize art and reference books. A flyer on the desk announces Monday night movies--tonight it is 'David Copperfield'. Along the walls floor to ceiling, like ivy grown over every inch up to the window and door casings, are books. This is a library, one feels, that knows what a library is for.

A tall bay window at the far end of the room lets in a countryside of light and air. In the window bay sits a rocking chair, stripe-padded, in a shaft of sunlight. Piles of the *New York Times Book Review* and the *New York Review of Books* are beside it. It is a feeling too smug to be told to sit there mellow in that sunlit bay reading the *Review* and, rocking softly, defusing diatribes of angry intellectuals--their arguments like brilliant death grips easing off your throat. 'They're smart, these guys,' you think, looking out the window to see an old timer going by in his truck, 'but not as smart as they think they are.'

Some children tumble down a narrow staircase from their library upstairs: five little girls all dressed--considering the general dress code of the town--quite up. They have a few balloons in tow, and parents. They have been, they announce to the librarian, to a birthday party and now are the richer for it by the treasures that they show her--some baubles and some hard cash.

The white-haired, smiling, chattering woman checks out some books for a stranger and stamps the cards. But this is, it seems, a somewhat courtly gesture. There are no fines, she says. And when the stranger wants to take along a *New York Review*, she spells out the Draconian nature of the West Tisbury Free Public Library circulation policy.

--Oh, those aren't checked out. Just bring it back when you're through with it. I think Milton and Henry have already seen that one anyway.

I leave, in love again, this time with a library.

On Alley's porch bulletin board amid announcements of Yoga classes and rides-to-New-York-wanted, a large REWARD sign, pink, reads WANTED: SANDPLAIN GERARDIA, and the tiny flower's infamous face looks at me, larger than life.

The Martha's Vineyard Garden Club is offering a $25 REWARD for information leading to the finding of the Sandplain Gerardia, *Agalinis acuta*, formerly known botanically as *Gerardia acuta*. A search committee has been formed.

The Sandplain blooms 'small as your little fingernail... for several weeks around August 25 to September 20.' It is September tenth. Fame and fortune can be mine--and on the Vineyard, too. I resolve to establish myself forever in island hearts and history by discovering the wily Sandplain. Too, I will be rich.

Places to look, the notice explains helpfully, are Chappaquiddick and the outwash plains along the southern part of the island. This information is discouraging. Chappy is big and what are outwash plains? Where is South, for that matter. The southern part of the island is the longest side of its triangular shape. It looks too big for combing for fingernail-size flowers. Dry sandplains, old dry fields and cemeteries, are also likely habitats.

The only place I understand without reservation as locus is cemeteries. But I don't especially want to crawl around in them. I look in our back yard--you never know, you know--but the Sandplain lacks sportsmanship and uncooperatively is not there. Island glory will have to come to me another way.

Still, Aunt Helen and I go over to Felix Neck, the wildlife sanctuary, to see what we can do to educate ourselves in island nature lore. The first lesson of this visit is that nowhere is safe.

We are gathering in the barn, seven women and a man, to take a wildflower walk. Big wild turkeys are pecking around the ground outside the window. One of the women, after watching the wild fowl intently for a moment, breaks our strangers' silence with a shrill and distinctly strange remark, considering the context.

--They say wild turkeys just taste so much better than the other ones, she says.

Another of the women laughs, I fear, rather outloud.

--Yes, I've heard that's true, says yet another woman.

But the first woman, seeing the expressions or studied lack of them on the faces of the other nature lovers, appeals to our guide for her defense.

--Well. Don't you ever experiment with one when it dies?

Ellen, who is leading us on our walk, says nicely no they don't, then points to a tree nearby.

--Fred lives there, she says. He's an orphan. He fell out of a tree when he was a baby and we raised him here. So he doesn't have a natural fear of humans.

Fred appears in a tree above us and greets us noisily. Then he flies over and lands on my head. Someone asks if Fred has friends of his own kind.

--Bluejays don't mate until spring, so this is the time of year for him to make some friends, says Ellen. Birds are friendlier at this time of year and form casual groups. It's an open society with migrants coming through, and they tend to accept one another more easily than they do in the spring when they have established their territory. Fred needs other birds so he can feed, not be driven away by the other birds all the time. He needs a mate.

Fred, apparently checking out his choices, leaves me for Aunt Helen, trying to take her scarf by one of its red stripes. Then he tries to get Mr. Langford's yellow hat. He stays with us for the rest of our walk, hopping from branch to shoulder, interjecting many remarks to help Ellen explain the nature of nature to us.

...

One of the carpenters giving the Town Hall a lift calls out to the other with impatience.

--Virgin land. Virgin land! What do they think they mean by virgin land? What are the standards of purity?

His tone suggests that he expects no answer, and he gets none. His criticism drops gently twenty feet to my ears as I pass by, trailing along the picket fence by the church across the street, kicking leaves on my way to the library.

I like him for sounding so crabby, and know he is referring to an ad a developer has run in the *Gazette*, a newspaper that recently used the word 'greed' in a big headline above a story about a developer. The right word is often sought and found and used in this community.

At the library, I am browsing in the stacks alongside a woman in a work shirt and jeans. The librarian calls to her.

--Eleanore, turn on the lights over there. You can't see a thing.

--No thanks, says Eleanore. I'm used to the dark.

--I thought you'd like a lot of light since you're a painter.

--Maybe, says Eleanore, that's why I don't do so well. You know.

--I don't like a lot of light, says the librarian. My husband is always coming in and turning the light on in the kitchen, and I tell him to turn it off. Men like a lot of light, I think. My mother always read with just a little light on by her, and my father would come in the house and turn on all the overhead lights.

--Reagan, Eleanore says, wanted soft lights for the debate.

--I thought he looked old. He has really gotten old, says the librarian.

--Mondale, too, says Eleanore. He looked awful, and all those bags under his eyes.

--Shelley Winters, says a small woman who has come in during the conversation, said that when she acted with Reagan twenty years ago he had gray hair.

--I don't think he dyes it, do you? says Eleanore.

--How could he not, says the librarian, if it was gray twenty years ago?

--I don't think he dyes it, says Eleanore.

--He must have a really good beautician, it does look so natural, says the small woman.

--Or maybe he uses that stuff Pete Rose uses, you know, that makes your hair turn slowly back. What's that stuff called? The librarian searches for the word.

--Grecian formula, says Eleanore.

--Grecian formula. If I used it, I don't know what would happen, says the librarian. My hair was blonde. It would probably turn it black or something awful.

--I was going to use it on my cat, says Eleanore, but I decided better not.

--Your hair is nice, natural. I was white when I was thirty. My daughter's hair is turning white now and she's just thirty.

--Did you see that little crippled cat they advertised in the paper yesterday? asks Eleanore.

--You know they have hundreds of cats down there, says the librarian.

--But this one was so cute. It was born with something wrong with its leg. I hope someone goes down and gets it.

--Why don't you? says the librarian. It would be good company for your cat.

--My kids would kill me.

Then Eleanore turns to address a silent stranger.

--You're so quiet. This is a funny conversation, isn't it? About cats and gray hair.

--And light, I say.

--You always hear funny conversations in here, says Eleanore. A lot of people live alone here, and sometimes this is the first time they've talked to anyone all day, other than to say 'get out,' or 'get down.'

...

Although it is the end of October, walking out one morning I am greeted by an air so gentle it caresses me, and I feel comforted as though I have just been wrapped in a favorite memory. The breeze smells sweet; tiny field sparrows sing briefly.

The day has dawned a bright, light gray with a horizon in view. Now the gray is deepening and moving closer to the house. Soon there will be no horizon. We are after all on this tiny island six miles off the Atlantic coast, at sea. And so we have sea weather.

We are into weather here, and I watch through the glass doors all morning for the predicted cold front to come up the road like a dog, which it often does. At eleven I go out and am assured by a breeze that the cold front is not here yet. Soon the fog rolls in at eye level and sits on the porch like a pillow.

The island is described in a celebrity-written travel piece this week as a microcosm of the great world. Maybe so, and maybe that is why I wouldn't give a nickel for most of the communities here. West Tisbury is the place, away from the touristy harbor towns of Vineyard Haven, Edgartown and Oak Bluffs. West Tisbury is a microcosm of a world that never was--at least in my experience. It is a utopia where all the men are able, all the women are reasonable, and all the Labradors drive their own pickups.

This town is foreign to the America I have known, in the most subtle ways that add up to a difference that makes a difference. People here feel keen about that difference, and when something particularly unworthy is happening in our country--for instance this Reagan landslide--they feel it all the more. The sigh on Alley's porch is the unarticulated question, *'what did you expect?'* And with a thumb gesture toward the mainland and an exasperated expression they say, with or without words, *'In America over there, they're doing it again.'*

I am alone here now in a house I have rented in West Tisbury. Aunt Helen has gone back to Kansas City, and I am trying to call my own bluff. My introspective self has my motherly self and my frivolous self roped off from the old life and corralled here in a sturdy post-and-beam construction house in the woods. We have a big deck. We have a fireplace. And we have virtually nothing of our own, nothing that ties us to that former life.

We have none of our favorite things about us: no piano, books, records, pictures. No scrapbooks.

Here I sit on someone else's chairs, sleep in someone else's beds, eat off someone else's dishes. There is no hit to be had off the great consumer drug called 'this is mine.' No part of me is identified with anything I own. And what happens? These foreign objects become treasures of not-mineness.

They are gracious and charming hosts; I admire them down to the very leaves and flowers of the unmatched plates. They are welcoming as if they have been waiting my arrival. I love these things because they are beautiful in themselves. I love them more because they are not mine.

My happiness here is irrational, which distinguishes it from pleasure, perhaps. This happiness seems sprung from a source within that has been tapped by solitude and by the loveliness of the sea-surrounded country town.

The sun is out and warm now. I could stretch myself out on the deck. I could do so nude. A celebrity-written photo book about the island shows the demimonde frolicking about the beaches bareass. They look okay, I guess, but not particularly natural, which would seem to be the idea. In fact they look pretty edgy as though the effort to be pleased with themselves is wearing. But this is not my problem. I am not a beautiful person summering here. I am a West Tisbury winter rental person, and baring my flaccid body here is no better an idea than, say, streaking Holden, Missouri would be.

And so I keep my socks--and jeans and shirt--on as I read on the deck in the afternoon sun, Brahms drifting over me into the brush and scrub oaks, on as beautiful a day as any life can hold.

My new friend Jane comes by. She has written a lot of racy books and made a lot of money at it. A mutual friend in New York told me to look her up when I got to the island, and I did. We are a nearly perfect odd couple.

She writes things I wouldn't be caught dead reading. I write things that don't make money. She can't see why I bother. She gives me some of her books, and I take a ginger look to see what made all this cash flow. I don't know what to say. I give her a couple of reviews and essays I've done and she knows what to say but has the grace not to say it. She screams when she sees me reading Milton or Proust or the *New York Review of Books*.

--The trouble with you is you don't read the *National Enquirer*!

We can't talk about junk, we can't talk about 'literature.' I try the *New York Times Book Review*, which seems pretty docile about following popular taste lately, not overly experimental or esoteric in the notions that it proffers. But Jane won't read criticism and forbids its mention in her presence.

Subjects she likes are her health, operations, vitamin therapy, astrology, real estate, and romantic involvements not her own. Her monologues are very funny; Jane always makes me laugh. Since I am incompetent on most of her subjects, I pick the one I know and cough up some accounts of some lighter affairs in an effort to amuse her.

--You're like a teenager! she screams.

--Well, you're jaded and heartless, I snap back.

She has most material things she wants, including property here. She once advertised with the eternally optimistic thousands who look for a mate through the personals. But that didn't work. I describe to her an American I met in Greece who wants to come visit me .

19

--He's heartless and mean spirited. Maybe you'd like him.

--Invite him, she says.

But I don't because I think she doesn't know what she's saying. And I'm afraid by the time he gets here she will change her mind and leave me stuck with him.

It is an odd friendship. And it grows.

A newcomer on the island scene in the fall, a thirty-year-old who dresses like a punk rocker and calls herself Lulu, wants to talk to successful Jane about her, Lulu's writing. She calls to ask Jane over for tea.

Jane, showing uncharacteristic bonhomie, goes. I can't believe she is going to talk about anything but herself. If Lulu can get her to talk about her, Lulu's, writing, I will give her, Lulu, credit.

A few days go by before I see Jane again. I ask about tea with Lulu.

--My God, Jane says, that woman talked nonstop for three hours. I almost collapsed and fell on the floor listening to her. She's rattling on about how she gets up at 4:30, writes for three hours, then lifts weights, then starts writing again and writes for twelve hours--or was it eighteen?--God.

--Sounds dire. You see any of this flood?

--She gave me a story.

--And?

--And what?

--Did you, are you going to look at it?

--I don't know.

Jane calls the next day.

--Well, I read her twenty-five pages. Nothing but this one screaming argument between children. And every exchange ends with an exclamation point. What drivel. I hated it. I don't know what I'm going to say to her now. God I hate this.

--You could give her some, you know, constructive suggestions.

--Ha. It's too awful. There's nowhere to wade in and start. Everything is wrong with it.

--Any description?

--None. All dialogue.

--Well, tell her it's a play.

--It's not a play.

--What does she know? I'm just trying to think of something you can say to her.

--I hate it.

--So tell her you hate it.

--I can't do that. I'll just tell her it's good.

--You can't do that.

--Us poor writers. We're all so fragile and hopeful.

--That is the truth.

--I dunno. You know what I'd like to do? I mean really

like to do? I'd like to walk up to her and sock her in the nose--blam!

It is at this moment that I know Jane has an interest in and a gift for literary criticism that we have not yet begun to explore.

...

One day we are sitting in my rough little house in the scrub oaks. Jane is eating an ice cream sandwich at one end of the table while I staple book envelopes at the other, running my one-book publishing empire, peddling basic journalism.

--I'd rather be sitting here with you than doing anything there is to do in New York, she says.

Then she starts on one of her amazing monologues, this one about her other, that is, former lives.

--They were all terrible, she says, terrible. Except for one. It was in the Netherlands or somewhere like that, and I was married to a solid little businessman. He was round. And I was round--blonde and buxom. And we had a bunch of children. It all took place in the dining room. The whole life.

--How do you know you really lived this life and didn't dream it, imagine it, make it up? You're a writer, you know.

She is used to my eighteenth century Reason. Instead of berating me, she smiles good naturedly.

--You're so *here*, so *this is it*. You're like a tree, an oak. You're like an oak.

--But you always say I'm like a teenager. So what am I

now? A teenage oak? How many children did you have anyway? What were their names?

Jane changes the subject. In her best loyal way, she has decided that an overeducated, unbelievably talkative poet-carpenter who worked on her house would like me. So she sets up a Sunday brunch for the three of us.

Fritz was there when I got there: tall, cheerful, intelligent, and most gratifyingly, considering what I had just been through lately, older than I. We had a nice day together, the three of us.

He drove us to the site of a great house he was working on--a frame only, a beautiful spare skeleton against the blue horizon high on a point of land above the sparkling sea. It was a Magritte-like wonder of scenes that could not be, and Fritz and I climbed over and around the stage-set house, catching views from different perspectives through the frame, breathing in the spectacular vistas, elated, shouting into the blue.

--Lay down your hammers men! This house will never look better than it does today!

Jane sat in the truck, pleading bad feet, but for whatever reason unwilling to clamber around construction sites talking to absent beings and shouting at the sea.

We all went to my house for coffee, and by late afternoon, as Jane dozed between Fritz's and my giddy cultural conversation, it was clear that he and I should be friends. When you find someone on the island you can talk to, that is, talk to, you do not just yawn and walk away. Besides winter was coming. And along about November--which it was--facing another frozen island winter, otherwise reasonable men have been known to fall deeply in love with any woman available, at least until Spring. Fritz was ready for a woman, and there I was. Verifiably the thing itself. A woman. And laughing at his jokes.

I really liked the man, liked the things he taught me about the trade and tools of building. The Japanese pull their planes, he said. Westerners push theirs, like luck.

I liked walking in the great dunes beyond Squibnocket with him, a dazzling, otherworldly landscape where we felt like the first explorers on the moon. I liked him for taking a look at me so placid from my new vegetarian regime and sizing things up immediately.

--What do you expect? You eat like a vegetable, you feel like a vegetable. Eat some food, woman.

But Fritz prided himself on several years' work on his character during which he had become his real rather than his former presumably objectional self. Who could help wondering about the lurking reality of the former self? How much awestruck admiration was appropriate?

There were other things about him that troubled me. There are always things about men who want to share my cage that trouble me. I can weasel my way, it is true, out of any long-term, life-share threat. But Fritz's qualities were, I thought, almost sufficient to make my side of the story sound reasonable.

One thing was that the gods had apparently spoken to him saying, 'You need an interest, Fritz, not just an interest to occupy your fertile mind on long winter nights, but an obsession that will serve to test the tedium threshold of your friends as you go on about it for hours nonstop, breathless--how about the history of film?'

Sometimes driving back from a companionable enough dinner or movie, I would catch myself nodding off in the truck, head bouncing perilously close to the windshield as he drew from the fabric of film lore its finest threads: who played in what with whom and where and when. And why me, I would wonder, snapping to. I will say this for him, that when I asked him to stop, he usually did.

Another thing I couldn't like was that he had no money: that is to say, no money. I think that after a certain age, given the advantage of a sound mind in a sound body, a man should keep a little buffer against the whims of fate.

But the other this-is-the-real-me feature of Fritz's act was the one I thought Jane might have been kind enough to advise me of before our first happy brunch. He had no teeth. I am not saying that in my hidebound bourgeois Weltanschauung the prospect of being intimate with a toothless man was difficult to consider. It was impossible. I have since visited many museums where I have noted that in almost no works of art do the subjects show their teeth. In cases of agony or ecstasy, however, teeth show up. Which affirmed a sensibility that resisted. I could do friendship, but not ecstacy. Dinner was hard enough.

I couldn't get over the idea that behind his talky exuberance lurked the thought that we would be lovers. But I knew it did. And when I went to Paris, here it came. I was followed by gifts that looked like they were from the Littlest Angel, and by letters elaborating his emotional progress in such great detail and in such a florid hand that it was impossible to understand. I kept thinking, 'but we weren't like *that*, we were *friends*.' Still, when he wrote of his travels and joyful intimacies with another woman, I was completely confused about his idea of courtship, and finally I lost all patience with him.

The thought had flickered from time to time on the island, 'well, maybe if there were some teeth, we could negotiate something here. Many women suffer boredom at a man's hands as Edith Wharton's poor Lily does, hoping for the honor of being bored by him for life.' And so on. But this faint line of thinking was eradicated by the flood of madness surging at me from across the sea. It is not his fault, I know, that the flowers sent on my birthday looked like a forest rather than a bouquet--a result of the dollar's strength against the franc, I suppose. But I felt violated by this ongoing assault and the most generous thought that remained about him was: this man is on some strange wave length.

When I came back to the island the next year, Fritz took me to lunch to tell me what a wonderful year he had had, living until recently with a 'wonderful, warm, responsive woman.' And it had all happened because he had fallen in love with me, he explained helpfully. Fritz did do this for me: he helped me to understand the emotions ascribed to the heroines of the 19th century novels--the ones who swoon with shock and offense when a man declares his devotion.

Aristotle, meanwhile, seemed my best ally and I found myself snapping at him: 'there is no cause in nature for this line of carrying on, Fritz. Stop it.'

Taking another tack, he leaned across the table and like the Paris taxi drivers, suggested he could take me out sometime since I was here alone. He could show me around, make my stay a little more pleasant. By this time I was ready to use Jane's literary criticism on him, and told him so. And so at last this strange unhinged friendship and romance ended. I think. Although God knows what's going on in Fritz's whirling dervish of a mind.

...

In October, after I have been on the island about six weeks, people are being pleasant to me but I am still very much an outsider in West Tisbury.

'We are dealing here,' I tell myself, 'not just with New Englanders, 'but with New Englanders who are also islanders--a double dose of insularity.' But I am so infatuated with West Tisbury, this last outpost of true civilization in the known world, that I know it is going to have to take me in sooner or later as one of its own.

At Alley's one day there is a strange, big, self-important looking car parked out front. The thing just fairly screams 'not an island car,' it is so different from the pick-ups and beat-up compacts everyone around here drives. (When people want you to know they are selling a reliable junk heap, the code phrase in the classifieds and on the bulletin board at Alley's is 'perfect island car.') It doesn't take any figuring at all to know I am looking at a politician's car. And it is not hard, inside Alley's, to pick out the driver. Here is this stocky, type-A guy in a brown polyester, waffle double-knit suit going on at Jim Alley at the post office in the back of the store.

--You can't represent them over there and these people too. There's just no way. You can't do it, he is saying.

Jim is absorbing the guy's constituency problems pleasantly enough from behind his barred window. (Jim usually keeps the bars between him and the people while Tony always raises them, getting more hangers-out. A lot of people on the island in winter have a lot of time to hang out.)
I squeeze by this plump brown suit to get to my mailbox.

--Good to see you. How you doin'? says the politician affably, looking me over pretty thoroughly as a potential vote.

--Fine thanks. You?

--O.K., thanks. Fine, thanks. Good to see you.

We are getting along as famously as all this when Jim to my surprise breaks in to spell us.

--Well, you'd better excuse me so I can get this mail sorted, or Helen will be mad at me.

And in a minute, the man is gone.

--Who's the politician? I ask. Jim names him.

--And?

--And what?

--And is he the good guys or the bad guys?

Jim, who has answered without flinching such questions as 'which way is North?' dodges this one.

--I don't know. I can't give political advice while I've got my federal hat on.

I am impressed by Jim's professionalism, and of course I don't care about the politician because all the way home all I can think of is that Jim spoke my name. I exist in West Tisbury! And I am just smiling like a fool as I turn up Old County road. I am still thinking about it when, hopping the steps onto my deck at home, I take a little extra leap at the top and yippee, 'I'm a citizen of West Tisbury!' And even when I go down to the Town Hall a few evenings later and Heidi registers me as a legitimate voter, it's an anticlimax to my big moment at Alley's when Jim Alley spoke my name.

...

A few weeks later Joanie's son is filling my tank when an older guy who has been leaning against his pickup walks over, opens my passenger side door and says a little too cheerfully, I think, that I've got some trouble.

--You've got a flat, doll. I've just been watching it go down.

You have to dislike a guy for this. I get out and look at it. It is not just a flat; it is flat.

--Could be, my angel of bad news says, tapping my tire, this ten-penny nail you've picked up.

--It's what I get for hanging out at construction sites.

--I'll put some air in it for you, says Joanie's boy, and they'll fix it for you down at Goodrich.

Goodrich is seven miles away, in Vineyard Haven. Kenny's Up-Island Service is behind Joanie's gas station, fifty feet away. Kenny's worked on my car, I am thinking, I-am-not-a-tourist.

--Can't Kenny do it? I ask.

--You mean here? No he doesn't do that. You could ask him.

--You've had that nail a while, says the bad news messenger, who won't be happy, I guess, until he gets his kick. It's just a bad day. You shoulda stayed in bed.

--I stayed as long as I could. It's 11:30.

--Shoulda stayed.

--It's not a bad day yet. Maybe Kenny will fix it, I say.

--It's Bill who's having the bad day, says the other guy pumping gas, gesturing at my tormenter.

A young woman drives in and calls out merrily to Bill.

--Well, gee whiz, Bill Payne. I see you got a young friend. I was following you down the road the other day and she was all over you, and I kept honking and yelling, 'Hey, papa! Hey, girl! That's my papa you're doing that to, girl!' But you just ignored me, like I wasn't there.

--Boy, says Bill. I don't know why you're all giving me such a bad time.

--We're just jealous, the guy who is not Joanie's son says, handing me my ticket to sign.

--There's not a finer man anywhere than Bill Payne, announces the young woman, with the air of an emcee at a roast, an event being recorded for posterity.

--Say, says Bill, I hear you on the radio saying, 'This is Bridget, and you aren't going out on this boat, people.' You sound mighty cute.

--That's me, calls Bridget, pulling away pleased. Cute.

I find Kenny in his William Booth shop: there is clutter everywhere and grease rags and tools and bemused car owners posing morose questions and a dazed dog in the middle of it all, emblematic as the one in the cartoons. As we walk back up to my car, Kenny asks if I have a real spare or one of those disgusting little paper things. When he sees my full-sized spare, he is gravely pleased.

--The new ones don't have those. And he looks at my car and me with reserved approbation.

--I can plug this for you, he says. And he rolls the offending tire into his shop and out of sight.

I walk to Alley's for the mail, and when I come back I don't see Kenny anywhere, so I sit in my car--which is now sitting square--reading the mail.

--You looking for me?

I look up at Kenny and think what an exotic-looking guy he is, with the beautiful features of some enviably successful racial mix.

--Hi Kenny. They told me you were gone.

--I'm just wandering around here. You owe me four dollars.

--Thanks. I'm all set then?

--You're rollin'.

I roll out thinking about how many worse things can happen to a person than having a flat. And to have a flat twenty feet from Kenny and have him confirm your new legitimate citizen status, too. I am not having a bad day, Bill. In fact, I have a letter from my son here, which makes it a banner day.

Bill's probably having a good day, too, what with that young girlfriend who is so fond of him and all.

It is a perfect day, actually, and Judy is in a terrific mood, chattering merrily at her post at Alley's behind the rich colors and smells of today's offerings: fall vegetables and Florida fruits, Diane's pot of soup steaming next to homemade rolls and Charlie's perfect coffee.

--I just took my lunch up the road and ate with Joanie, says Judy. It was great. Eat your hearts out summer people--here it is November, beautiful weather, and no crowds. Ha!

Judy's lost twenty-six pounds on her diet, and Friday is her day off her diet so she can have anything she wants. She's looking great, and I say so. Judy who pretty much beams anyway, beams brighter.

--What's this to keep us healthy today?

--Tomato-bean-barley, says Judy. I take some and Judy asks if I had yesterday's soup.

--I can't remember. The turnip chowder? That was great.

--No, the cabbage-beef. I couldn't have it because of the meat, but you should've tasted it.

--Next time. Something to look forward to with hope, I say.

And out I go, then turn and come right back in, realizing that if it is Friday, it is *Gazette* day.

--How could I forget? I hand over the thirty-five cents for the week's news on the island.

--Everyone's doing that today, says Judy, taking the money with a flourish. I don't know if it's the beautiful day or my brilliant personality that's got 'em all so distracted.

--Got to be a little of both.

...

I have to step over Lambert on the way out, that disorienting animal, that major personage of the town. The first time you see Lambert you're not sure what you're looking at. An enormous mound of thick, dark fur is spread across six planks of the porch, blocking your path. Is it a dog or a cat? Perhaps it is two cats. It doesn't move. Is it a trapper's take for the season?

Lambert will unfurl slowly, revealing that he is some cat: big, black-faced, white-whiskered, and very New England. Lambert is impressed by nothing. Luxuriating in the sun, he displaces his space in such a way that he may as well have one of those Do Not Even Think About Parking Here signs over him.

A sign on the door does say that dogs should stay out because Lambert the cat eats dogs. And enormous dogs and bouncing puppies skirt Lambert without asking any questions, challenging any assumptions.

Human citizens step over him with a neighborly but polite 'Good morning, Lambert.' He accepts this homage without comment.

Often Lambert will amble into the store and into his dinner sack, putting quite a lot of himself into the 50-pound bag of food that he himself pulls down from the shelf and tears open when it is time to do so. His corner --where baskets of onions and potatoes meet the ice-cream freezer with the newspapers on top--is a busy corner, and you would think Lambert would get stepped on a lot. But he does not get stepped on at all. Even I have never stumbled over Lambert. He is a major cat. Wherever he is, he is what is happening.

He can be accident prone, and when he broke his leg not long back, all the Alley's regulars signed his cast.

One day, out of the blue, Lambert is all spiffed up. He looks like he is going out on the town, he is so fresh and, well, fluffy--and Lambert is no way a fluffy cat. What is going on?

The Gazette has the story. Someone left an oil can in the parking lot of Alley's, half-full. Lambert, who is in charge of the premises, went to inspect and ended with an oil bath. Charlie gave him eight rounds with the Dawn soap, and--*voila*!--the new Lambert. The newspaper reporter scolded the irresponsible oil-changer for endangering Lambert's health, and put people on notice to throw their hazardous waste out properly. Lambert had no comment.

...

On Monday and Wednesday mornings now I go into the West Tisbury Free Public Library to help Margaret Barnes, the librarian, discard books from the tiny library's bulging collection. Books crowd into the old wood shelves that have the tiny room surrounded floor to ceiling.

Our rule is that a book goes 1)if it has not been checked out during the past five years, 2)if it is not in the Sears directory of classic library holdings, and 3)if both Mickey (that's Margaret when you know her better) and I can bear to see it go. Spinoza has not been checked out in twenty years, but he is just going to have to keep his chin up. We're not throwing him out. Plato and Aristotle are doing a little better; each has been checked out twice within the past five years. Thirty theosophy books, all crisp and eager for converts, show the undisturbed lines of books that have never been opened. They were gifts to the library. Gifts account for quite a number of the library's holdings, complicating the battle of the bulge for Mickey and tending rather more toward zeal than readability.

A book is saved if it fails to meet any of our three conditions. But if it meets them all, it is gone. Being asked to throw out books is like being asked to help drown kittens. I value books, even those I do not like.

After a month of this, I am beginning to enjoy throwing out some of these things, and am less and less inclined to let one stay if the third condition, that we can bear to see it go, is its only salvation. I am getting to actually dislike some sorts of books. It is, for example, becoming more and more difficult for crackpot religious books to find a haven here.

After all, the books we take out of the collection are going to the book sale where they will find a home with someone who wants them--a better fate than sitting unread on our shelves for twenty years, I rationalize shamelessly.

My friend David writes that he knows now what to tell our mutual friends in Kansas City when they ask what I am doing.

--I tell them, he says, that you're throwing the Bible out of the West Tisbury Library.

...

St. Augustine remarks that learning without learning to love God is vain, and that people who do so are no better than those silly women who are always learning but never achieving wisdom.

Well. Sisters unite.

Too, I would like to see these other women who are silly in this particular way. At home in Kansas City, I have always been considered a little *other* for my constant carrying on with books--and the friends with whom I share this addiction are men.

But they fill the West Tisbury library today: women who love to learn. I like to think we share a passion for learning to know good, that we are not like those silly men who pursue learning only if it serves their lust for power and fame, for being right and being in charge.

I am hunched over the I's now--IMAGINATION, IMMIGRANTS, INDEPENDENCE, INDIANS,--working on a subject headings list. The tiny library is full of women; that is, four or five of us. A pretty blonde in jeans and an old blue-green sweatshirt runs in, a battered old black hard back in her hand. She lands by Mickey at the table.

--I want this book.

--What is it? Mickey asks.

--It's a history of English literature, and it's wonderful. Could you find out what it's worth? I'd like to buy it.

One of the regulars comes in looking for another P.D. James mystery and Mickey goes to help her while the woman in green answers my questions.

--It's like Henry Adams, she says. The style is elegant, and, oh, it's beautiful. I think I had to read it in college twenty years ago, but I didn't appreciate it then.

She hands me the book. It is Taine's *History of English Literature*. Published in 1879, the book has pages ragged and brown with age and solid with tiny print. It has been sitting on our shelves for twenty years, in storage for the past ten. No one has checked it out in all that time. Some books, like some of us, require very particular attention from very specific people. A sudden lover has come to call for Taine. Oh, will Mickey let her have him? Surely she will.

I look over at Mickey who is absorbed in the search for the new P.D. James, oblivious to the soap opera churning in my heart. I ask the woman if she is doing a project.

--No, she says, I just read the new Chaucer life-and-times book, and got interested in Norman French, and I've been reading about it. The chapter here on the influence of Norman English is really clear, and exciting.

A buoyant white-haired woman in jeans comes in seeking numbers. She is hooked on numbers now, she says, correspondence and sequence. Mickey talks with her a while.

Then as though she had never left the table or the conversation, she comes back and without hesitation, says the words that seal the fate of lovers.

--Just take the book, Sally. We'll find out what it's worth later.

And Sally is out the door at a run, Taine in her arms. Mickey looks after her a minute, then turns to me in her direct, no-nonsense way.

--That's what books are for, she says.

...

Reporting to volunteer duty on a bright October day, one in a string of perhaps twenty-five glorious ones we have enjoyed, I find Mickey and two other women conducting a League of Women Voters committee meeting. The eldest woman and her husband have a time-honored celebrity in West Tisbury as bright young stars in Roosevelt's administration who lasted through to Truman's.

They are on agenda item three, tax bracketing.

--I don't know what you're talking about, says Mickey.

--Have you ever done your income tax?

--No.

--Well... and the Roosevelt woman explains what happens to make bracketing a losing proposition for some people so that you go into a higher bracket and you lose all the income you've gained. Mickey says oh and after some discussion they decide that it is harder on the poor than on the rich, so they will recommend against it.

Items four and five are about deficit spending.

--Pure Keynes, says the woman, priming the pump.

When line item veto, number six, comes up, the Roosevelt-Truman woman recalls that Truman could veto items individually, that when a whole budget was good except for one thing, he could and often would strike it out. Like that. They decide to recommend in favor of line-item veto.

The league opposes higher excise taxes. But when they come to proposed increases on liquor and tobacco, they discuss it a bit, deciding that 'even if we taxed these so-called bad things, it wouldn't raise much money.' So they stick to their principles against raising taxes.

In a printed questionnaire going out to members, they include this recognition that their members are not a bunch of go-along, get-alongers.

--Note: There is no box for 'don't know' or 'stupid question, I won't answer.' If you feel that way, just leave it blank.

...

Dawn backlights these florid coral floral curtains with the message 'it is day,' and I lie here admiring the rich spangles of gold that play across them before getting up to pull the curtains open so the sun can warm the room in its full force.

Out of the warm nuzzle of pillows and comforters and into fifty flat chill degrees, I feel not the cold but the purity and innocence of this indoor camp out. Outside, a warm breeze lifts my scarf and thrills me with the daily morning news this fall, that it is warmer outside than inside. I store the lawn chairs upstairs for the winter, and stash more logs into their shelter. It is almost December.

The wood smells sweet and musty. Bare handed, I think of other hands across the island, working to get walls and roofs up before the winter. The day is good for the carpenters. We will not have many more days like this this year.

Doors open, the house invites the morning in as I fix vegetables and rice, trying to work with patience and humility as instructed in a holistic health book left here by another tenant, because, it says, the miracle of growth is slow and patient. I eat standing, walking around, looking at the gray and white clouds that drift slowly to the west. I love to eat this food and in this way, another freedom I didn't know I didn't have. I wonder who among my friends at home will let me stand up at their dinners or listen to my benediction of the broccoli.

Robert J. is talking on the radio, planning the program for next Thanksgiving, which makes me turn and look at the radio. Who believes that tomorrow will come? He is planning for tomorrow a year away, in the most deliberate of manners, so that I almost believe with him that another Thanksgiving will come. No one sounds more assured of the world, his way, than Robert J., a blessing and a curse.

This institution of a man, this omnipresent WGBH morning host is not one of your excited radio announcers. In fact, if you're beginning to get in gear when he comes on, he can shift you right back into neutral. His halting drone suggests a man talking in his sleep. Is he awake? Is he still there? A listener unaccustomed to his unusual style cannot imagine, during the frequent three- or four-second pauses between words, what has happened. Has the station gone off the air? Has Robert J. nodded off and fallen to the floor? Searching the radio dial for WGBH Boston any morning of the week--for he is there and not there every morning--you can easily turn right past during one of his ponderous silences.

If you do not know what is going on at seven, when he starts his program with five minutes of nature sounds, featuring vague, distant chirpings, you may think you haven't got a station at all but a Bob White out in the brush, and pretty soon you're out wandering around the grounds, scanning the branches for bird life and missing the morning news.

Robert J. plays a teaser for next Thanksgiving from volume two of Hymns Triumphant. When the choir sings, 'Come ye thankful people come,' I am in tears--as I knew I would be the minute he announced it--thinking of my family, of how often we have sung that song together gathered around my mother or my aunt at the piano, of my father, dead, my sister, dead. I go to look at a box of food I am sending to my son, as though the sausages and cheeses there will somehow alleviate the pain of our family misfortunes and failures. I telephone my mother and ask her to be sure to invite Joel to stay over Thanksgiving when he will be out of the dorm and homeless.

For the first time I understand the words 'all is safely gathered in 'ere the winter storms begin' in a visceral way, and soon I am back out gathering more wood into the dry shelter, relishing the triumphant serenity of being in the natural world. Satisfaction radiates through the task into my miraculously useful hands.

I sit in the sun after the work is done, feeling a clarity and goodness and a gratitude that must approach what is called grace.

At night I discover how to build a fire, and for the benefit of those whose technical expertise robs them of the joys of incompetence, here it is:

Begin with green and wet wood which will keep you ginger busy twenty minutes stuffing wads of six-week-old Sunday Times under it until you tear off an article entitled, say, 'The Last Castrato,' and sit back to read what otherwise you would have missed of the distracting variations on the human theme.

Go out, after a while, after you have faced it that this is not going to work, to seek seasoned wood by moonlight. Meet there a pleasant rabbit rabbiting about and a ruffed Grouse with whom you will exchange the time of night. Look up. See Venus and Saturn rising purely by a cradle moon. Breathe deep the brilliant starlight; think how this tiny island shines now in the sea.

Bring in one log too long to fit the fireplace. Poke in a perpetual pattern at it; this compulsion makes a rasping math, a music that will lead you into meditation on the verdant popping sparks fresh over firecoals. When the log breaks through sometime later, you come back into focus and put the now two logs in order on the now good warming fire.

Pull up the big chair, close. Get *David Copperfield* and make his journey yours on this December island night before the fire.

...

Snow is on the ground. The holiday season is on us now, and we are gathered in the green-bedecked West Tisbury Congregational church to hear the gifted young guitarist deliver his advertised sensitive interpretations and brilliant technique. He is doing fine, easing from a Bach sarabande into a minuet when a young man in glasses carrying a camera with a foot-long lens comes scrunching up the center aisle as if in creeping combat. Or perhaps it is a duckwalking event of which the audience for what was thought to be music is unaware.

40

He advances on all threes, camera held high, clicking one handed, to left front below the stage. He finishes off a roll and to reload scoots center to sit Buddha-like directly beneath the guitarist. He snaps upward through another roll into a sensitive face that is showing signs of strain.

On the third roll, a balding hero rises from the fourth row, walks upright to the photographer, speaks a complete thought to him and returns to his seat. One feels this was a sentence that had two words in it, no more than four. The photographer desists. He sits still for the rest of the concert. Perhaps the hero turned him into stone; there is joy in thinking so.

But then this was a day to keep the surly self at home--a beautiful day enough to be sure, but just the kind of pushy day that makes the sullen heart resist. The internal dialogue goes something like this: Beautiful day. Should want to go for a walk, I suppose. Even the Victorian doll ladies all corseted up in Dickens take an occasional turn about the garden or go visiting in town from time to time, put one foot in front of the other.

But I would really rather stay in bed. I don't know, despite all the studies of exercise and jogging, that the primary research has been done here, reported in the literature. That is, I don't know that definitive evidence has been advanced that man, the species, should get out of bed at all.

Did not Aristotle hold that the natural state of any body is at rest?

Has not Pascal taught us that all the evil in the world comes from man's inability to remain quietly in his room?

Let's face it. Looking at the world as it goes now, the lesson for our species easily could be, *we should have stayed in bed.*

--Sometimes we stumble, sometimes we fall, says Jack, quoting the Bible, I suppose, but always adding, *and those seem to be the choices.*

--Who's next? said Bruce, anticipating a new infidelity during a frenetically erotic era in our crowd in Kansas City years ago.

--Who's left? said David, grabbing his best girl and walking out.

I am not saying I'm depressed or out of touch, but I just read the Boston Globe for thirty minutes without noticing that it was a November issue. Is it my fault that the world turns so that distinguishing one day's from another's news does not come naturally? Or that the island winter nights begin at four o'clock and then go on forever?

...

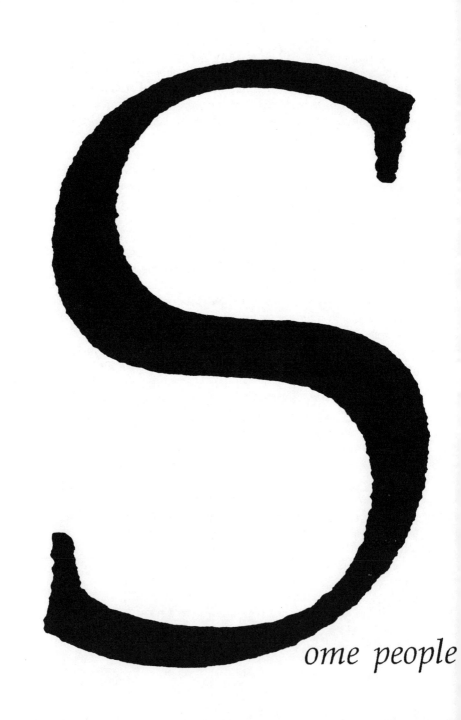

ome people

it is said, get so island-bound that the day comes when they cannot leave at all. Just cannot leave. It has taken me into its quiet winter ways, worked sea-changes in me. I've evolved into a quieter creature, one that does not drink or smoke, that eats brown rice and vegetables, meditates. I am thinner, calmer, better acquainted with self and solitude. And I am ready for a change.

The palest J.M.W. Turner sunrise lights the day, and gray gives way to pink and gold over white water as the ferry crosses. Then we're set loose: a caravan of free citizens heading up route 28, on the road again, on terra firma, into the world.

Robert J. talks to me on the radio, and I know he is droning these same slow words to the morning light in my house in the woods. I hardly know which place I am, it has been such a ritual padding around the cold house each morning for months now to the sound of his drugged delivery. His words form around the hermit me that has been left behind in this take-off for Paris.

At the airport in New York I ask a White Rabbit-like man in a red coat if he can tell if Joel has made the plane from Kansas City. At last report, Joel had not found his passport or his tickets. I've been trying not to think about Joel. Now the man taps at his computer console for a few seconds, looks up and says the words. 'He's on.'

An hour later Joel emerges from the mass of people in the waiting room, a miracle, my son, a man. When did this happen? And has he always given off such energy and light? I can't get over him.

At Orly we see Robin walking toward us down the long concourse in her red dress and coat, tawny from the Côte d'Azur sun, a sea of faces turning in her wake. She is so beautiful and full of joy that Joel and I just look at each other and laugh. Then we are in a three-way hug of triumph: we are here! We all are here. I am crying of course, and Robin is, but manful Joel just beams upon the women. I think of Jack with a terrible brief sadness for him, for us, that he is not here.

45

Although I have researched a small library of travel literature and even written some hotels, the fact is that with my no-plan planning we have no place to lay the collective joyful family head. I've got a list. We try, in our excitement, to look it over rationally, but end by trying the first two hotel names on the list. This means talking on the phone in French. I am terrified.

Robin takes pity, goes to the phone, and demonstrates that her junior year in Nice has not been spent entirely at the beach. She reports that the first place is a youth hostel that will take any mother that can take it; the second is the Hotel Saint André des Arts, about to become a legend in our lives. It has been recommended by my friend Terry as a real French hotel (no elevator, bathroom in the hall) run by a pair of cultured and talkative brothers, the messieurs LeGoubin.

The taxi that takes us and our eight bags in costs ten dollars including tip; we are agape at how far the money goes at ten francs to the dollar. I feel guilty, but more than that grateful, for without this stroke of economic grace, we would not be here at all.

We have all been to Paris before, which only intensifies the joy of seeing it now. To see Paris is always to be dumbstruck with renewed infatuation. As the gray elegance of facades gathers around us on the ride into the center of the old city, we breathe the magic that it is to be here.

Turning into the rue Saint André des Arts, we could be arriving in Oz. Delighted by the jumble of small walking streets that make up the neighborhood, of which the rue Saint André is the most perpetually in a state of public carrying on, we tumble out of the taxi and into the black-and-white tiled reception hall of the hotel. We stand there dazed. M. Philippe LeGoubin takes one look at us and advises us briskly that we are the Ashmores who have just telephoned, that our room is on the fourth floor, and that, as there is no elevator, we will walk up. And so for the first time, we walk up the hundred steps to the room that will be our home for the next month: room thirty-two.

We baptize it with a great deal of white Bordeaux and singing. (How quickly my island virtues left me and how glad I was to see them go.) We'll sing in the streets, we say, and become rich and famous. Then Robin and I go to bed to dream of fame and fortune. And Joel goes out to see what's happenin' and to jam.

...

We are hanging listless about the room in various states of lag the next afternoon. We have been to the Right Bank. We have seen the prices. We huddle in our room, afraid the money might get out and go there. We are in this crisis of feeble wills when there is a knock at the door and Phillip walks in.

I have seen him in the morning at breakfast, a social occasion at which I do not excel and which I therefore usually do not attend. But there I was, and there he was; and I perceived him through my morning ire--this skinny California poseur at the reception desk in his Levis and Vuarnets speaking chummily to M. Henri in a preposterous British accent. I hated him on sight.

Now here he is standing in our room.

He sits down, plays a few really nice chords on the guitar, looks at us sunk around the room and laughs. Then he is singing 'I could while away the hours conversin' with the flowers, consultin' with the rain...' and we are laughing and delighted, and we have Phillip in our lives. It seems quite wonderful and natural. I can conjure that moment any time in any place and be back in room thirty-two, and there sits Phillip in his white jacket and turquoise shirt, his handsome face cocked over his guitar, his dark head swinging slightly as he sings to us of a heart all full of pain, the charm flying off of him in sparks.

He lives down the hall in one of the tiny garret rooms the brothers LeGoubin keep for poets, painters and musicians. The rooms rent for about seventy francs a night and tend to attract long-term residents like Frederick, the black Frenchman whose story is that he was an accountant but who now verifiably sits abstracted in his room quietly strumming a guitar borrowed from Phillip and singing like Nat King Cole. There is Pascal, the hotel's only truly Parisian resident: a poet, philosopher and science-fiction writer both wise and naïve far beyond his twenty-two years. Pascal's French resembles my English in that no one ever understands what he is saying in his native tongue he talks so fast.

Both Pascal and Frederick are devoted to the other resident of our floor, Suzanne, a poet from Seattle with blonde hair that hangs nearly to her waist. Serious and calm and competent, Suzanne works daily in the Paris libraries and jogs most evenings in the Luxembourg Gardens nearby.

The other floors of the hotel are thick with models and photographers, some of whom are amiable enough. But there is no floor like the top floor for sheer lunatic camaraderie. Last year, M. Henri informs us, the top floor was occupied exclusively by writers, so that when he came up the stairs and heard the terrific busy little clatter of the keys, he would think of elves tapping in Santa's workshop. M. Henri, far from disdaining his poor poets, is proud of them. (The French have virtues Americans forget. Or underrate.) *Quel homme, M. Henri!* What a guy!

One of the artists in residence of whom M. Henri is most protective is Phillip, the musician, our new friend.

The day we came and Joel went out to scope the scene, he found Phillip standing in the hotel doorway, guitar in hand.

--Hey man, said Joel, you wanna jam? Phillip, who like so many Americans in Paris fears and loathes other Americans in Paris, was so startled by this direct attack that he agreed.

--Sure. Meet me here at midnight.

--Meanwhile, he said, I heard all this singing and playing in your room, and I thought, well, Joel, you rascal, with two women in there partying. You sounded like you were having a great time, and I wanted to come too. When Joel came down to meet me, I asked him what was going on.

--Oh, said Joel. That's just my sister and my mom.

--I couldn't wait, says Phil, to see you.

Seeing him now that it isn't morning and now that his Vuarnets are folded in his pocket, I realize what a handsome man he is--a sort of Richard Gere and Warren Beatty rolled together and then rolled out very thin. As we get to know him, I will begin to see him as a combination of two other gentlemen as well: Don Quixote and Don Juan.

After we have known him perhaps a week, he has an idea.

--I'd like to be adopted here, please. I want to be a part of this family.

To hear his family stories, the ones that are not funny, he needs us. So when Jack calls from Houston on Christmas eve, we all crowd into the tiny phone booth off the lobby where we are gathered when the call comes in, to tell him the good news.

--A miracle, dear Jack. Remember how you always wanted another child? Well, here he is. And Phillip sings for his new father over the Paris-Houston lines, never mind that he is twenty-six, that Jack and I have been divorced for twelve years.

--Come on, says Phillip, taking control. Joel and I will go play in the metro, and then we'll go to dinner.

When they come back and I come down to meet them, Robin and Joel already in the lobby, say, 'look Ma! another Phillip!' and another dark haired, very fair and lovely man leaps up laughing.

--Aha, the mother! he says, and bounds across the room, knocking me back out the door as he grabs my hand and kisses it. I think, struggling to keep my balance in my boots, that I have never seen anything quite like Luis-Felipe before. I am right. I haven't.

--Let's go, says Joel.

--*Allons-y*, say Robin and Luis. And so we are off on the first of many orchestrated rambles--what we learn to call 'going to dinner.'

Immediately on stepping out the door of the hotel it becomes clear that the primary object, whatever it is, is not to get there. A sort of hanging-out in transit, the object clearly is to be there. There is much starting and stopping involved in being there--weaving through the Buci market, arrested by glorious tulips the hue of dusty roses and brilliant roses themselves tulip-red and tulip-yellow, by the startling blue *fleurs de lis* against the white foil of the heavily flocked Christmas trees. Among the art galleries along the rue de Seine, the delicate curves of a painted Japanese face mask lure us to the closer study discovery of a man and woman engaged in exotic but unmistakable coitus. Being there involves a lot of waiting: waiting for Luis to go into the *tabac* and return with cigarettes for all of us to bum off one another--all cigarettes in Paris are, effectively, in the public domain--waiting until we find Joel who has lingered at his art education, waiting for Phillip who has struck up conversation with a pair of beautiful Swedish *au pairs* he knows, their hot pink-and-black Paris plastic earrings dangling over their sweet fresh cheeks along with wispy blond curls.

As soon as everyone is gathered who has rambled out of range and Phillip is satisfied that we are proceeding in a generally agreed upon direction, he swings his guitar into life and sings us along our threading way--now Indian file, now in twos or fives--through the brisk December evening crowds of St. Germain--our lanky piper, making even the dour Paris faces break into smiles at his easy good nature. Soon we are not so much walking as dancing and singing along, acting up in general and laughing especially at Luis, a natural clown who can and does outdo anyone who ever has gone out to enjoy the streets of Paris.

--My people, says Luis, gesturing to the crowd around us, these are my people. Then he mimics Phillip mouthing silent words behind him or singing in an exaggerated operatic style.

He cavorts ahead with a leap and spin and then stops around the next corner to hunch into his green trench coat and light a cigarette, leering at us coldly sidelong with the air of a street tough as we parade by. He teases Robin, offers advice to Joel as a young man entering the world. He drops back with the mother, to brood in his beautiful Napoleonic profile under dark straight hair about the nature of suffering in the world.

--Mom, says Robin. Don't talk French to Luis. He can't understand you. She sweetly does not add, 'who could?'

We pause before a window full of bright neon objects and a pompous in-crowd that has gathered to ignore them in the name of Art and, by unspoken agreement, plunge into the art opening. Luis works his way deep into the crowd while we others accept champagne; then he turns and works his way back to us through the solid crush, pulling faces at us in playful disdain of the neon art and its French yuppie patrons.

51

We arrive finally at a restaurant called the Beaux Arts, and with a great deal of gesturing and shouting in several languages, Phillip and Luis determine that it is the wrong Beaux Arts, so we set off again after quite a lot more conversation in another direction or two.

It takes about thirty minutes more of street participation, art appreciation and restaurant rejection before we lap back around to a charming little two-story restaurant with white tablecloths and roses. Luis balks at the bourgeois pretension, but we outnumber him, and that very night we have dinner.

One thing Luis could have used on those evenings was a shepherd's crook; he worried if someone strayed seriously out of range, and went to get them. Usually it was Phillip, an accomplished *flâneur*, lingering past patience at a window or a girl.

...

The next day, Joel and Phillip practice some songs, almost instantly have an act together, and disappear into the subway to sing. I imagine this to be a thrilling moment in my son's sheltered life. A few trips with Phillip when he descends into this perfect hell, sets me straight.

Singing in the metro in the winter is not glamorous. Surreal faces bounce dull and staring through efforts to please them with music. Stifled, ruined subterranean air closes in. You cannot wear an overcoat without roasting; so you must make your way through the bitter cold of the streets above shivering in a sweater. Winter is a time of year to be got through for people who make their living on the streets of Paris. To be broke in Paris in the winter, to be earning one's bread and shelter one day at a time, is not even very edifying. It is what is called in common parlance an experience. But this celebrated thing--as in 'won't that be an *experience*!--has harsh edges in reality.

Even so, when Phillip and Joel come back two hours later with a load of coins, they dump it on the table and, after counting it out and dividing the take between them with the precision of an audit, shove it back together again into a mountain of promise and say we're all going out.

--Come on, we're taking everyone to the movies.
And we all troop off to see 'Cotton Club' on them.

How selfless of the American manchild--and what generosity in the street musician to entertain their friends and family with all they have. Yet Phillip's version of our Paris Christmas meeting is simple.

--You saved my life, he says, who brought us to life.

Movies are a passion with Parisians rich and poor alike. In spite of the harsh reality for those who live hand-to-mouth, and because of this reality, they will have their evenings before the shining screen. The crowds--the French do not stand in lines--are there each night in a shoving sea of eager escapees before each twinkling marquee on the boulevards.
They believe in movies in the way that children do.

--Yes, Luis says after 'Cotton Club', that is the way America is: violent, racist, money-mad.

--No, I say, like Prufrock, it is not like that at all. Not at all. That is the movies. That was a movie about gangsters and racism, very romantic, in a time long past. The reality is much less...uh, lurid...uh, I'm searching for a word...much less extreme..

Luis does not understand me or believe me, and I am not sure I believe myself.
Later, he makes fish and crepes and noodles for us all, including a German girl who has arrived in Paris and in the hotel Saint André des Arts lobby without a cent. After dinner he brings out a photo album with photos of his family in Portugal: his beautiful, elegant parents, his

mother holding him as a baby, him as a small serious handsome child, the family home grand as a castle and surrounded by lush green. Him in his young he-man body at the beach, and most recently him on a night out on the town with friends in Lisbon. One of the friends, one he is holding the arm of in one of the photos, is a vivacious young woman, pregnant and laughing.

--My family had everything, says Luis. Now I have nothing. But he has something. The woman is a girlfriend. The baby is his, theirs.

He speaks of his father with a kind of concerned patience.

--She was an opera singer, but now she lives by the sea and she is a painter.

--He, says Phillip. You mean he. Your father is a he. And everyone laughs.

--He, says Luis. We ask him about the baby.

--She is bee-oo-iful, he says. Bee-oo-i-ful.

--Beautiful, says Phillip. Bee-oo-ti-ful. I thought the baby was a boy.

--Bee-oo-ti-ful, says Luis. She is a boy, and she is bee-oo-i-ful. Beau-iful sounds more beau-iful than beautiful.

Luis loves his language and his country; often at night very very late in the hotel lobby he and Joseph, another Brazilian Portuguese, and another countryman or two will be gathered to talk and talk and talk their common language, the language of heroic early navigational history.

They are still exploring from the sound of it, with passion in every syllable of what for all we know may be talk about the weather.

Luis pours his heart fully into each move, each thought. Everything Portuguese is best, he believes it in his heart.

--Portuguese shoes, they are the best, he says as we pass a shoe store. Or Portuguese shirts, or Portuguese wine.

--Helen, it is the best.

Once when we are watching an old movie with the recurrent line 'I wonder what's doing in Portugal,' Phillip and I begin to say it, and Luis says that nothing is doing in Portugal, that is why he's here.

--In that time, in the twenties and thirties, Lisbon was like Paris, full of life, he says. Now it is finished.

The people in the movie want to go to a bullfight in Lisbon.

--Ah, says Luis, brightening, Portuguese bullfighting. It is the best. Because they do not kill the bulls.

A little later, when Phillip is trying out his gift for languages on a beautiful young Italian woman who has come into the hotel lobby, he tells her in his fearless Italian that Portuguese bullfighting is the best kind because they do not *muerde* the bulls. The girl laughs and mimics biting her wrist.

--*No, no mordere!* she says. You do not mean they do not bite the bulls. You mean they do not make them dead-- *no morte*. They do not kill them.

Nothing linguistic daunts Phillip. He talks to everyone in every language. His forte, to speak true, is *des choses banales*, that is, small talk--in French, Italian, Spanish, German, Swedish, Danish and Japanese. Because he is so clearly laughing at himself when he goes into one of his 'Hi, how're ya doin'? how long you been here? what are you studying? where are you going now?' spiels, people laugh with him and talk to him. I have never seen anyone refuse to talk to him on the street. He has them laughing in a moment no matter who they are--a pair of shy Japanese girls, a family of dour Swedes, a troop of Spanish street singers in their grand capes and hats.

He watches me when I am reading a book in French.

--I can't read a word of it, he says.

But he is fluent in any conversation, even with the literary Henri, while I find myself stammering to express even the simplest thought. *Un creme*, I thought I had learned to say so that I would get a coffee with cream. But once when I have been in Paris several months, I order *un creme* and the guy comes back with *un timbre*, a postage stamp.

Phillip's gift for language seems so natural to him that he does not understand that all of us don't share it.

--Of course you do, he says impatiently, you just aren't trying.

...

A round the world, there must be many bars like the Mazet, our local watering hole here on the rue Saint André des Arts, but I have missed them. The neighborhood bar, while justly cherished as a haven of cheerful conviviality, is also a preserve of the upright ape at his territorial worst and it is a wonder that anyone goes into one who does not have to. It is a challenge, at the least, to understand why anyone would go into one thinking to relax. To vivify his vocabulary of insults, yes; to perfect the arc of her left hook, maybe. But to relax, no.

Of course there are those who must clock in at the neighborhood bar: the regulars. It is their place, their society and recreation. As some people light up their lives with handball, and others with slam dancing, bar regulars charge their systems with the energizing complications of extended drink and conversation--sometimes lifelong, like marriage. They have no choice really. The bar is to them habitat and habit, a powerful clutch, a headlock. They are expected. Their failure to arrive would upset the natural order and confound the other animals.

But of those who seek out such places--where they do not belong--what can be said? Do they not know the meaning of the word *local*? Have they forgotten the film 'Easy Rider'?

And yet these naïve adventurers will seek them out. From the seedy commercial strips outside Kansas City to the sandy hills surrounding Kamloops; from the dusty square of San Miguel d'Allende to the jumbled maze of Saint Germain des Prés, such people track the locals to their watering holes and walk onto the scene. The locals look up from their pool tables and pinball machines, and there they are: the strangers. Fresh prey, raw meat.

It does not daunt these peripatetic strangers to be run out of a black club at knifepoint amid shouted accusations of 'narc!' or to be doused by the drink of a raving old woman in a London pub shouting 'jews!' or to be implored while sidling out of a gay club in Manhattan, 'Oh, darling, don't leave, come with me.'

They remember only the good times, like the time the troop of *federales* in San Miguel befriended them, carried them home that night and came to escort them to brunch the Sunday morning after.

Yet nothing in one's experience of taverns on this planet is adequate preparation for the Mazet.

The Mazet's clientele is international. So far, so exotic. But it is a sort of countercultural anti-U.N., for it brings people of all nations together where they may sit down peacefully and discuss the world for about twenty seconds before they fly at one another's throats in fury.

The men--and the Mazet, like all bars, is a male preserve--are drifters from all over; many make their living on the streets as musicians, and some of them are musicians. The neighborhood is global, the bonhomie of the bar as tentative as a powder keg.

The first time we walked by it, I was terrified at the sight. One look that surging rabble of angry, self-anointed outcasts, and the warning light flashed on.

--No way I'm ever going in there, I said.

--Really? said my steadfast young companions. And in they went, while the mother scurried out of the Cour du Commerce alley and into the relative safety of our pleasantly zany home across the street.

--What is that place? I ask Phillip.

--Oh that's the buskers' bar, he says, beaming into my scowl. All the street musicians from England and America hang out there. Some French and German ones too. It's lovely. It's the office.

Joel and Robin cross the street an hour later, and I ask how it has gone.

--Yuk, says Robin.

58

--Ugh, says Joel. And they charge thirty francs for a beer.

The Mazet faces our hotel; our rooms look down on it, or certainly I do, marveling at the second principle of thermodynamics in action there. Like all systems, it is proceeding headlong toward randomness and disorder, that is, toward entropy. But yet, the very essence of the place is disorder in the most unruly sense. All that negative masculine energy--how much farther can it proceed? Is the Mazet entropy incarnate, the word made flesh? I ponder this beyond the patience of my friends.

--Meet me at the Mazet, Phillip says, trying to see how far he can push me.

--Let's call from the Mazet. You know all the hotels add thirty percent to long distance calls.

And so it is that I go into the Mazet. I greet 1985 standing in the Mazet with dear Luis who pretends at midnight not to know me while twenty other men grab me. I eat lunch there, which now seems an almost physical impossibility. I become a sort of irregular at the Mazet.

It is all probably because of Jeannot, the bartender. He kissed me when Phillip introduced us and whenever I came in after, soft-stamping my cheek with this sign of acceptance and protection. In gratitude, perhaps, I fell in love with Jeannot.

--Ask him if he's married, I nudge Phillip one day.

--*Tellement!* says Jeannot. Roughly translated this means, am I ever! So that idea was out.

But Jeannot was the one to have for your friend in the Mazet. His presence calmed that scene of a daily dozen unpleasant encounters. A drunk Algerian spitting insults at

Americans, a frothing German grabbing a woman to dance and refusing to release her, a slick street black demanding money. These are among the charms of the Mazet ameliorated by the knowledge that Jeannot is there.

And Jeannot is always there, surefooted as the trainer in the cage. He wears the Paris bartender's uniform: red vest, white shirt, black pants and unflappable demeanor. He steadies the animals when they get violent, using among other Orthodox methods, that of the swift kick in the pants that can propel a man halfway up the street. This is a last-resort tactic, used only after reason has been exhausted. For two Parisians to exhaust a conversation on any topic takes a good long time, but even the French know that the reasoning abilities of a man who has just had fourteen drinks are not extensive.

Jeannot, big-armed, round-faced, a shock of blondish hair forever across one eye, works at a steady pace from opening time until two or three every morning when--if we are still up--we see him from our window, patiently stacking the chairs in the alley, his carriage brisk as though the day has just begun. He occasionally shows a slight weariness behind the eyes, as though he has seen enough of this. But, to borrow from the Latin, the bastards do not ever really get the indomitable Jeannot down.

Phillip in the Mazet with his forties' elegance looks like Fred Astaire among an international rabble of army deserters. He is all black and white and crisp and witty; they are rough in army brown or London green, bearded, heavy-sweatered, and wired to the touch with explosive anger.

(Phillip showed up in my New York Times the other day as model for what Aquascutum is calling their 'forties classic look,' and I would just like to say that although I saw him first and noted it before they did, the fact is indisputable; it is his look.)

--Everyone has to have a look in Paris, says Phillip, looking me over with regret.

What makes the few civilized people who go into the Mazet do so is a puzzle to me. It is not the music, which is usually pretty bad. Vulgarity and mediocrity dominate the scene there as (as Proust has taught us) they do anywhere. So the good musicians are seldom heard.

But there are what even Mother would call nice people in the Mazet. Phillip's friends the ebullient Tommy Tortellini (né Rogers) and the refreshing Neil Berrymen, they are there. And Clive, the courteous and manful Welshman who has just chosen the career of busker over that of teacher. Ari and Andy, the California student writers, gentle and intelligent, often write at Mazet tables, waiting artfully to be teased by Jandi and Lee, their season's torments. These bright young women are protégées of Odile Hellier whose Village Voice, the brilliant newcomer English bookstore in Paris, has left the shoddy, reverend Shakespeare & Co. in the dust. (*Protégées* means they enjoy the privilege of work without the sullying insult of pay.) Such people do come to the Mazet.

When I ask one of Phillip's girlfriends, a beautiful French schoolgirl of sixteen with a moon face and hair to her waist (she is his season's torment), why she would come into such a place, she gestures toward a man at a table in the back. Her answer is one word, his name.

--Jacques.

Jacques--*old Jacques* as the others call him--appears to be ancient as the mariner, but he is probably not much over fifty. He has the long, gray unwashed look of an Old Testament prophet, and he is in the Mazet all day every day except Sunday when it is closed. He creates a little clearing of civilization in the jungle of the Mazet where younger men and women gather around him to talk. He has a gentle manner, a ready smile, and a reputation for being a compatriot of Sartre. He will not tell people his surname.

--I am going to the library and I am going to look you up, Andy says to him one day.

--You will find me, says Jacques.

'Under what entry,' I wonder. 'Jacques'? I often long to talk to Jacques but am afraid to because my spoken French is ludicrous and because I comprehend practically nothing that a native speaker says in French.

--But he speaks English, Phillip says.

As more encouragement to make the move now, Phillip advises me that Jacques has worn the same thing every day for at least a year and has only just changed clothes a month or so ago.

--So this would be a good time, he says expectantly.

But something about Jacques is too good for stumbling banalities. A conversation without sureness of language would be awkward and ridiculous.

So I will leave Paris hoping to talk to Jacques when my French gets better. Or when I get comfortable in the Mazet. Whichever comes first.

...

If the Mazet represents the left bank in its history of teeming street life, the good brothers LeGoubin sustain its tradition of a rich and proud culture. On the day we announce our intention to do tourist duty in earnest, M. Henri, M. Philippe's brother, is at the reception desk. He delivers not only the requested directions to the Jeu de Paume but also the precise address along the way of each important moment in cultural history: where each artist and writer and political figure has lived, created famous work, done famous deeds or died along our path. When he is through with us, we feel that it will be appropriate not to walk through these hallowed quarters but to make our humble way in the posture of pilgrims, on our knees.

When we go to see the Beaubourg, the Centre Pompidou, the museum of contemporary art, we are assured that whatever our gifts for getting lost (mine are extensive; my internal compass points to perfect South, and I once got lost on the Staten Island ferry), we cannot miss it.

An enormous and world-famous architectural disaster or success depending on who's doing the talking, it is not just a building but an anomaly in central Paris. It has exterior elevators and brightly painted exterior plumbing and heating pipes. It is also a festival-in-progress. Fire eaters and street singers, fortune tellers and street troupes enacting dramas all surround it, as do playful sculpture gardens and fountains.

Robin and I go to find it on a soft lovely winter Sunday morning. We step inside Notre Dame to gape at the glorious rose window above a sea of worshippers. Then, our taste for stained-glass windows whetted, we pay a visit to the miracle of Gothic light and air called Sainte Chapelle, that great sustained glass Bible-story board.

We make it to the right bank and, following directions, soon are facing a large glass and aluminum construction that seems to be several stories of going on. On the top floor, signs announce *Maison des Arts*, and *Maison de la Poésie*, so we sniff around to see what we have found. The only exhibition we can find is called Creative Photography, and it is a major disappointment: a number of large rooms filled with the sort of affected and manipulated nonsense they were doing back at the Kansas City Art Institute in the seventies. This is the world-famous Beaubourg? Oh, please. We wander home confused. If anyone is more confused than we, it is M. Henri when we report in.

Phillip who has no emotional investment in the Beaubourg thinks the situation very droll and turns to M. Henri with the air of a concerned culture monger.

--So. The Pompidou is nothing but some old photographs of Kansas, then? he says.

It takes us two more tries before we find the Beaubourg with the help of Phil's friend, and now Robin's, Brad, who has been a street musician in the style of Phillip--which is to say a good one--and who is good at business, too. He has just made what is described to us enthusiastically by his friends as 'a pile' in California real estate and has returned to Paris for exactly such purposes as leading beautiful college girls to art.

On the day I set out on a quest for volume one of *À la recherche du temps perdu*, M. Henri gives me marching orders, and within an hour I have landed a beautiful 1954 Pléiade edition and returned to show him what treasure his intelligence has unearthed. He reaches for it, approves it with several meaningful French sounds, and pages through to a favorite passage, the one in which Swann, after the suffering he has undergone at Odette's design, becomes happily immoral again. M. Henri reads:

...avec cette muflerie intermittente qui reparaissait chez lui dès qu'il n'était plus malheureux et que baissait du même coup le niveau de sa moralité, il s'ecria en lui-même:<< Dire que j'ai gâché des années de ma vie, que j'ai voulu mourir, que j'ai eu mon plus grand amour, pour une femme qui ne me plaisait pas, qui n'était pas mon genre!>>

...with the old, intermittent caddishness which reappeared in him when he was no longer unhappy and his moral standards dropped accordingly, he exclaimed to himself: "To think that I've wasted years of my life, that I've longed to die, that I've experienced my greatest love, for a woman who didn't appeal to me, who wasn't even my type!"
(--Kilmartin translation, Random House, NY 1981)

He quizzes me about Faulkner and Fitzgerald, his *Americains preferés*. *'Feesjural,'* he says. *'Who?'* I say. I feel that I am flunking this pop test and try to steer him onto Joyce and Yeats, some ground where I can find footing. As he returns M. Proust into my hands, I wonder, does this man know every passage in every book in every language? M. Henri just smiles his elfin smile as in a kind of benediction, and goes back to his reading.

One day he comes to visit us in our rooms and proceeds, like Kit Smart praying in St. James park, to rout the company. With his brilliant, perfect, lightning-fast, Parisian discourse, he is a challenge of the highest order. I am ashamed for myself and for my country as one by one Phillip and Joel and Robin and various hangers on make their excuses and head for the street. His literary passion is beyond them, love him as they do for all the other virtues of civilization that meet in M. Henri.

...

Christmas is on its way, and we have tried to shop, God knows. But this trip *is* our present. Cash-poor, we are reduced to play. Robin lies on the bed in room thirty-two, talking French to the telephone, ordering a few small gifts sent up from room service for our friends.

--Des cadeaux, s'il vous plait, she says. *Peut-on envoyer des petits cadeaux de Noel?* Could one send up a few small gifts for Christmas? She has her hand on the receiver, so she is not actually talking to anyone.

We have gone shopping today, Robin and Joel and I, setting out this morning with earnest intention. But we have wandered off instead, under M. Henri's spell, to the Orangerie and then into the sixteenth to see the Monets at the Musée Marmottan. Walking through a little park on the way, we have discovered a cache of these tiny, elegant French persons--four and five-year-olds that look like miniature Renoirs--playing ball or riding furry burros or skating on a small pavilion in the center of the park. So we have had to sit a while and watch them. Then we have walked downstairs at the Marmottan and into a stunning moment of being faced with a roomful of Monets. Reeling from this visual overload, we have failed to see anything to covet in the shops along the boulevards St. Michel or St. Germain. We have taken a headlong, back-to-the-barn course for the Pub St. Germain and snuggled cozy into the now familiar dark booths for onion soup. Ah, home.

Many gifts are ours today, but nothing we can carry in our hands. We must have some things, though, and so as we collapse into the beds once more, Robin telephones room service.

--Allo, allo? Ah, oui. Des petits cadeaux, s'il vous plait, pour notres amis. Some gifts, please for our friends.

We like the idea of this preposterous request in a hotel that has no elevator, no room service, and certainly no staff of shoppers waiting at our beck. Robin and I fall into giggles and shortly into sleep. Joel goes out to jam.

When we wake, we decide on dinner in our room. This is a triumph of the human spirit over the physical world. Because nothing is simple, Robin and Joel begin by going out to Porte de Clignancourt to get a chicken and to correct Joel's wardrobe.

--That ski jacket, Phillip says, screams 'American!'

He thinks it more subtle to dress so that people must judge one's nationality by one's shoes--and we will spend hours in the Buci Bar playing at that.

But just now there is the matter of Joel's camouflage and of the chicken. Joel returns from market wrapped in a regulation Paris gray wool coat, and Robin totes a fine, fat chicken wrapped in paper with a pound of fries. It's grand, we all agree, but it is not enough. So Phil and Joel descend into the market to get some wine and cheese and bread before the market folds its tents at seven o'clock. Robin calls after them out the window, her voice failing to reach them in the last minute Buci crowd. So she runs down again and up the hundred stairs with lettuce, avocadoes, candles, flowers and cookies.

I put the pink silk frazzled shawl that keeps shoulders warm on cool evenings and toes warm on chilly nights, onto the table where it imitates a perfect doughty Victorian tablecloth. We make salad in the cookie tin and bring butter and flatware left from breakfasts in off the window ledge, along with the Clementines we have hung there in their sack.

Our dinner party is the toast of Paris--well anyway of us, and we have congratulated ourselves several times around and started singing when the phone rings. It is Luis. We have forgotten him. He is working at the desk tonight. So we go down to sit with him for the late hours, drinking wine and coffee, singing and talking among ourselves and anyone gregarious enough to join us.

On Christmas eve day we are out the door at the crack of dawn, which is to say before noon, once more trying to shop.

Over this city that is itself a celebration every day, spread lightly as spun silver, an air of winter celebration hovers. All of Paris is decked out in Christmas wonders: exquisite pastries, brilliant fruits and flowers, intricate, elegant toys and knickknacks fill the shining shop windows. Violent birds and beasts hang in the markets dressed in nothing but their tails for dinner.

We cannot cook a goose in our hotel room. So we gather all that we can carry of small glory in our arms: rich croissants, *pains au chocolate, tartes aux pommes,* quiches, plump golden pears and startling oranges, and a magnum of good champagne.

Joel stays with us, but he complains about everything. I hear myself in this debased, placating whine trying to humor him.

--What's the trouble, honey?

--I'm bummin', he says, and keeps his secret sorrow to himself. Meanwhile, he keeps complaining loud and rude.

Robin, in a glow of Christmas cheer, smiles through her croissant at his back.

--I'd like to kill him, she says merrily.

That evening as we dress for dinner, Joel is still glowering.

--Let's open the champagne, says Robin.

--No, not yet. We've got to wait for Phil, I say.

Which solves the mystery of Joel's anger on the spot.

--I don't want everything we do decided by where Phillip is, he says, saying it.

--I want you to be happy more than anything in the world, I say.

--That's more like it, Joel says. And from that moment on he seems o.k.

We bat away at some Christmas carols in the lobby, people from various countries wandering through and teaching us bits of national favorites, and Luis cooks rabbit in the tiny kitchen for a growing crowd. Suzanne our poet neighbor joins us, and she and I start talking about poets. Phillip eyes us with grave distrust.

Robin and I go out for more champagne and on the way back come upon a big, beautiful Christmas tree abandoned in the gutter. We drag it home and are followed in our spectacle by a pair of utterly drunk young men, one German and one Swede.

Once inside, the interlopers become aggressive; their language and demands send the women skittering upstairs. Suzanne and I are pleased to have the chance to speak of poetry where we will disrupt no normal conversation.

--I can't stand it when you talk like that; it's so pretentious, so boring, says Phil.

This is how we know our conversation is considered by some people abnormal. So Suzanne and I will take ourselves out to dinner every now and then to talk like that to our hearts' content in the privacy of the great Parisian public discourse.

Luis has gone to shower and get wine. He misses the invasion of the barbarians entirely for which we all are grateful. He has the day before grabbed the throat of a gendarme who had decided to arrest Phillip for playing in the metro.

--It wasn't really helpful, Phillip says, in fact it was insane. But they have come home unscathed and with a stronger bond between them.

When I come down to see if the coast is clear, it is not. Joel is squared off with the meaner looking of the two men, and Phillip is standing at his side and rather professorially trying to clarify the confusion.

--No. He said 'get the cups,' not 'get the cops.'

Joel is looking startled. Then the Swede reels and growls at him.

--Go ahead, make my day.

Joel and Phil and I all laugh, which is not politic. But the conversation peaks at this unpleasantry, and soon the gentlemen callers have staggered out the door and into Christmas.

Luis serves dinner at midnight with the best wine, Portuguese, and it is not until Phil has nodded off on Robin's shoulder that we notice it is three o'clock and time to say Merry Christmas and goodnight.

...

Phillip is practicing with a band tonight, preparing for his debut on French television. Luis comes tearing up the stairs two at a time and bursts in the door.

--The mother, where is the mother? We must go out to dinner!

Robin wakes from her evening nap and comes into the room rubbing her eyes. Her hair cascades about her face, around her shoulders.

--Look, says Luis, lifting her hair in gentle admiration, how your beauty is on you now, Robin.

He strums quietly on the guitar until Joel has returned from jamming, and then he leads us all around the corner to the jam-packed Greek.

This restaurant has a name, perhaps the *Orestia*, and it is on a block with at least two other large, visible Greek restaurants. But it is called by all the locals simply 'the Greek,' as in 'Let's go to the Greek.'

A long room, full to bursting with the rumpled intense black-clad people of the quarter and a smattering, always, of rather more substantial and alarmed to find themselves there foreign citizens, the Greek is as tumultuous a dining-out event as anyone could desire.

Long banquet-style tables cover the room wall to wall, with only the suggestion of an aisle through the middle where exuberant waiters bounce among customers, buoyant as rubber duckies in a stream. Nothing slows them, for where every inch is obstacle, obstacle is no consideration.

--*Combien?* they shout by way of greeting.

They don't care how many you are; they just want you to know they see you there. If you replied 'one hundred,' they wouldn't flinch. They would simply shout as they always do at dinner time, '*En haut!*' Upstairs.

--*En haut!*

We climb the narrow winding staircase where people go haltingly but the floating waiters waft right by. We emerge in a high-ceilinged room as tumultuous as the one below. A place is made for us, miraculous as the parting of the sea.

Joel looks the menu over and decides he can't decide. Who can? It looks like a page edited by Proust: the handwritten margin notes outweigh the printed words.

Luis takes charge.

--Have the *tsatziki*.

--The what? says Joel. What is it?

--The *tsatziki*. It is good, Luis says. You will like it.

--But what is it?

--Have it. You will like it.

--Funny how much you look like Al Pacino, bud. Is this an offer I can't refuse?

Luis orders *tsatziki, souvlakia, moussaka* and *Boutari*--the Greek Bordeaux--along with plattered chicken, steak and fries. It is delicious, all of it. Joel likes it.

After the waiter tallies up the bill on the white paper tablecloth, shouting down the line at each of us what we had, quick and lucid as a Macintosh, Luis and I throw strange, beautiful money into a pile in the center of the table until Luis announces it is enough. Now, he says, we must go to the movies.

Robin and Joel have other plans, so Luis and I pull our mufflers across our faces against the cold night wind and crowd purposefully toward the marquee of the cinema on the boulevard St. Michel nearby. What are we trying to see? 'Maria's Lovers.'

I steal a quick look at Luis to see what sort of man this really is. He looks at just this moment entirely responsible and sane, and besides 'Maria's Lovers' is sold out. So I relax.

We see a very odd film with some actors I've never seen before named Hill and Spencer bumbling around Rio. Even in no translation, we are able to determine that it is not a major work. Still, Luis assures me that I know these American film stars. A check with my popular culture experts yields familiar patient stares. *How clueless can you be, Mom?*

After the film Luis leads me to a brasserie that is just at one o'clock beginning to fill up. He speaks about his mother's and father's opera careers, now finished. Luis himself is like opera incarnate--absurd, sublime, and tragi-comic. Every notion, every motion is exaggerated, passionate: his motherly nurturing as he fixes dinner for us all, his macho god-the-father act as he orders us around and watches over us.

Luis will grow exasperated with me as we learn to know each other.

--Why do you think so much? Yes always thinking. You must learn to feel. Helen, you must learn to smell.

My great affection for the wonderful Luis will be marred only by fits of fury when he begins to treat me publicly the way a southern European man treats a woman he is close to: as though she does not exist.

But at just this moment I don't have a clue that things are going to get very complicated, a favorite Luis phrase. I know a few days later when he comes skipping up the hundred stairs--fifty to him--calling my name like someone coming home after long absence. Then I know. The rush is unmistakable. I am so startled; it is as though someone has struck me, and I just sit there thinking, 'Oh wait a minute here.'

But right now we're going to find Phillip and Robin and Joel to see what they are up to. We find them all asleep at three o'clock. We have outlasted them, bested youth tonight.

...

'Good morning, mama.' I hear this sweet sound each day along with Joel's growling 'Hey, Mom.' And I am mindful of my fortune, waking to Paris rooftops and my children. But now, today, Robin and Joel are going to Amsterdam, then back through Paris to Nice.

We must keep room thirty-two, that is rooms thirty-two, and so Phillip moves into the other of our rooms while they are gone. This moving operation means carrying from down the hall two doors everything he owns. I watch solemnly fascinated as he carries in his worldly goods.

This is the inventory: a pair of levis and the folding Vuarnets; a pair of black cord slacks and seven shirts; a navy blazer and a heavy white linen suit; a pair of black suede loafers, some boxer shorts and socks; a folding toothbrush, a blue plastic case of designer soap, a razor; two P.G. Wodehouse novels, one pocket French dictionary, one *Plan de Paris*, some cassette tapes, a modeling portfolio, a bag of snapshots, and one guitar.

--That's it? I ask.

--That's it, says Phil. This is how I live.

I am dumbstruck with admiration. This is how a man should live. For years I have kept a Chinese woodcut above my bed: of naked Eve-like women, with the legend, 'Possess nothing, own none; nakedly come, nakedly go.' And here it is in action. This is better than the Halston list for packing light.

I think of our eight suitcases, the sixty cartons stored at home with furniture for eight rooms. The piano! How can anyone own a piano? I have had to have it moved three times this year. In brief, I think, I want to be like Phillip.

He is the perfect roommate: quiet, clean, considerate and amusing. He pays his way with a determination that brings to mind Mr. Deasy, the headmaster in *Ulysses*, speaking to Stephen of Shakespeare.

'--He knew what money was, Mr. Deasy said. He made money. A poet but an Englishman too. Do you know what is the pride of the English? Do you know what is the proudest word you will ever hear from an English-man's mouth? [....]

--That on his empire, Stephen said, the sun never sets.

--Ba! Mr. Deasy cried. That's not English. A French Celt said that. He tapped his savingsbox against his thumbnail.

--I will tell you, he said solemnly, what is his proudest boast. *I paid my way.*

Good man, good man.'

A man of no attachments in the world, Phillip will be my best friend in Paris. He will give me what no one ever has, and what no money can buy: a life I could not have entered without him--of Paris streets and bars and people of every kind; a life of luxury and poverty, loyalty and betrayal, but most of all of music. I wished that he were older; I wished that he and Luis could be combined. Now that would be, I think, the perfect man. Perfect for what exactly I cannot say, except for me.

I am in love again, this time with a hyphenated man.

...

Snow! It is snowing in Paris. Flakes as big as sand dollars drift over the rooftops and onto bold French noses. Luis and Phillip gather handsful from the ledge and throw snowballs at the girls below.

They have spent the day at Paris modeling agencies, the two of them and Joachin, Phil's big, blond German friend and former roommate. Phil says it took the three of them to do it: Joachin to provide a foil, and Luis to threaten everyone, while he himself tried to look hard-to-get.

--Give me a hug, says Phillip, rushing into the room. I'm going to survive the winter! I've got a job. And new shoes, see?

Robin and Joel leave tonight for Nice. Phil resists a shower of phone calls from women with dinner invitations and goes with me to take them to the station. The slippery walks are treacherous, and no one in Paris knows how to walk or drive in snow.

--The whole city is on its bum, says Phillip, and then falls flat on his.

Joel performs a flying stuntman routine, skid-sliding back down the Cour du Commerce alley to get his wily passport which is in his suitcase all along. After we have sung the travelers off at the Gare de Lyon with 'The Sunny Side of the Street', Phil and I go to visit Ellen, a friend from home.

She is six floors up in four rooms on the rue St. Laurent just by the Gare de l'Est. We scale the steep stairs to the door, gasping with our last breath into a pair of Rocky Horror lips that recall the Bijou theatre back home, where Jack has educated my children in uncommon things.

Ellen is in a spirited battle with the vicissitudes of life in the city of light. The washing machine has been flooding the place for days, she says, but now is fixed she hopes. The stove is acting up, and the light in the kitchen goes out repeatedly. But we can see and smell the beautiful dinner emerging from the chaos. She assigns Phil the duty of being tall and forcing reason on the light bulb.

She sends me to the living room with my champagne. Eric discovers his evening's work of riding back and forth across my black patents on his tricycle. I am thinking that with Ellen occupied and Phillip hanging from the light bulb, I could settle things with Eric. But no, really, better not. Besides there's Max the dog there looking at me, and he looks like he would tell.

When Phillip asks if he can play an old Burton Cummings album, Ellen tapes it for him. The two Paris residents enjoy complaining of the Paris bureaucrats, comparing notes. It is agreed that the French so enjoy a passionate exchange on any subject with anyone that if you will stand up to a French bureaucrat long enough, demonstrate that you will fight him to the end, he will out of respect and deference to such spirit let you win. I have seen Phillip do this, with terrier tenacity, outarguing metro guards and gendarmes in their own language.

Ellen has managed to get working papers, using this method, because, as she explains, she had to have them. She has created a business for herself, teaching English to executives. She came to Paris on her own ten years ago, decided to have a child, chose a man to be the father, and here is Eric, age three. Her independence and strength of will are almost tangible personal effects.

She feeds us a sumptuous dinner, everything a tribute to the art of living well, and when the traditional New Year's cake is cut, she crunches on a plastic lizard that augurs good fortune in the coming year.

Max begs for cake and gets some. Eric is merry in his high chair and smiles at me so sweetly that I know there will be no revenge.

...

We're dressed to kill and heading for the right bank, Luis and Phillip and I. Emerging from the wide steps of the metro into the Bourse, we rotate around one another like out-of-orbit planets seeking direction. An extravagantly thin girl in purple head to toe--her hair is purple and her shoes and everything between that we can see--walks straight into Luis who bows and gestures for her to pass with a mellifluous, 'madame.'

--Where are we? Phillip asks her. I mean, where is the rue de Richelieu?

--But you are here, she points to the sign, amused.

We cross beneath the great gray columns of the Bourse, the temple of the stock exchange of Paris, and find what we are looking for on an adjacent street. The Hollywood Savoy, an 'American-style nightclub,' sits posh and shining on the otherwise dark, quiet street. Phillip, after his Paris television debut on P.M. magazine, has come to audition.

We peer over the cafe' curtains like street urchins in a Renoir film watching the wealthy gorge themselves. We pull back to look one another in the eye, comrades before the battle or the team before the play. Luis assumes his imperial Napoleonic air. Phil takes on the look he uses each year at the Cannes festival, when he gains entry with the claim, 'I am an actor.' He is, he explains, you see, when he is saying that. I try to look as bored as possible. Armed thus, we make our entrance.

The maitre d' buys this preposterous act and, removing a *reservée* sign from the best table, seats us near the piano. We are surrounded by large parties of substantial citizens in elegant attire. A certain heartiness, a will to have a good time or else, makes them seem more American than French. But they are French all right. It is early, nine o'clock, and so we order what dinner we have francs for.

The mannequin piano player nods and smiles over his tedious cocktail rendition of that all-time albatross of a cocktail song, 'I left my heart in San Francisco.' I gulp my Graves and counsel Phillip.

--A piece of cake, if that's the competition.

Luis will not address the notion that this is music, and when the piano player rises and goes into a babbling, idiotic patter that is meant to be a welcome, Phillip and I regret the fact that he speaks English. If he would speak any other language, I'd probably think he was amusing, though Phillip and Luis would know better. The French pay no attention to him, but we watch him closely because he is the man Phillip must talk to. We have another drink.

The mannequin introduces the evening's feature act: a trio with a singer from Seattle. Wait until I tell Suzanne. This woman is a show-stopper for sure, the incarnation of

Dr. Frank N. Furter in the Rocky Horror picture show. (Why *that* again?) Her black lace creeps above her thighs, above the subject it is meant to cover. She towers above us with a fixed red Rocky Horror smile. She sings enthusiastically and tugs her skirt down. Her little black veiled hat gets all askew.

--She has no subtlety, no range, no variation, says Luis. In short, she cannot sing.

I speak up for the courage and the will such people have in place of talent, and Phillip goes to find the mannequin. We see him approach the bar in his best James Bond stride and we laugh. He flashes us this 'please don't make me laugh' look and speaks to the little man in charge. He comes back agitated.

--The piano, he says, the piano. He wants to know if I play the piano.

--What did you say?

--I said I play guitar. But he said no, he needs piano.

--This is true, says Luis, attacking his salad. He needs very much piano.

--But you don't play piano, I say. Do you?

--Yes. Well sort of. Once. A long time ago. I might be able to.

--You told him yes, says Luis.

--Oh, gosh. I've got to find a piano, says Phil.

--When's your audition? I ask.

--Tuesday, says Phillip. Today is...

--Today is Saturday, says Luis, fixing Phillip in his best godfather gaze.

Back home in the snug lobby of the Hotel Saint André des Arts, Luis teaches Phillip *fado* chords and sings the traditional music of his country with all his heart as if to dispel the horror of the evening's music from his mind. Joseph tries to teach me a Portuguese waltz in French.

--*Non, petits pas, petits pas,* he laughs at me until I make small steps to move along with him.

Phillip and I go upstairs at about two o'clock. We have been there a few minutes when the phone rings.

--You must, Luis says, come down and listen.

--Luis, we just came up.

--Come down. You must come listen.

--To what, Luis? To what? It's two-fifteen.

When we walk back into the lobby, it is to find Joseph and Luis huddled over a small tape player as though it were a beer, listening intently. Tears are streaming down Luis's face, and his beatific smile breaks through on seeing us.

--You see, you see, he says, the greatest Portuguese poet! And he speaks the poem along with the recorded voice, his hand upon upon his heart.

I cannot understand a word of course, and of course I do not need to.

...

80

It may be illegal to beg on the streets of Paris, but it is not forbidden. And what is not forbidden is allowed, you see. And so a large number of the local citizens earn money on the streets of Paris with their hands or cups or caps out.

The requests are varied, as are the causes. People give. One learns to carry francs and half-francs in an outside pocket.

The humblest cause on the street to which one will be asked to donate is a beggar in a stupor, a heap beside the wall in the subterranean maze of the metro. He is bent over a scrawled sign, *'J'ai faim.'* I am hungry. He does not look up.

An Indian woman wrapped in a print sari that looks like it has seen many years and streets, is seated in the metro walkway too, a baby on her lap; a diminutive seven-year-old stands at her side with her tiny hand out. They are accomplished beggars; also accomplished pickpockets. You can give them something, or you can let them take it. It is entirely up to you.

More enterprising beggars approach you on the street and ask for money, some with a specific amount requested for a specific purpose, as though they have been to fund-raising workshops along with the Common Cause and Smithsonian development officers.

--Could you give me five francs for a metro ticket?

Never mind that a metro ticket costs two, it is the specified amount and purpose that work on, for instance, me.

Our American friend Terry, in Paris 'on sabbatical and full salary,' as he says excusing his prodigious generosity to me and Phillip, is leading me through the small shops on rue Quatre Vents. He stops by an old woman I have not even noticed and presses a ten-franc piece into her hand. I ask him why he did that, when she did not even ask him or make any gesture toward him.

--Ah, he says. But she is always here. And I always give her something.

--Why her? There are so many.

Terry, an exceptional man who freely admits that his own French is superior to that of most native speakers, values language above perhaps all other things.

--Because I like her, he says. Because when she first asked me almost a year ago, she used the subjunctive and she used it correctly.

On the stairs of the Odéon metro, dark activists impede pedestrians with placards showing mutilated Nicaraguans--like so many grotesque family snapshots on large album pages. I can give money but am too terrified by the violence of the photos to record my name for them.

A *clochard* who has laid him out unceremoniously upon the narrow sidewalk of the rue de l'Ancienne Comédie is not begging. He is not awake. He is comfortable, citizens assure alarmed American visitors who wish to have him picked up and taken somewhere to be fixed with workshops and counseling. He is lying on a grate above the underground hot water pipes, and dignity forbids making a fuss over him.

But what about his bare hands and feet that stick out cracked dry and frozen in the bitter winter afternoon?

--We gave him gloves once long ago, Madame LeGoubin, M. Henri's beautiful, sweet wife, says gently, when asked about him later. But he would not wear them.

At midnight on New Year's Day of 1985, snow is falling softly as Luis and Phillip and I make our way back from dinner at the tiny Deux Dragons on the rue Monsieur le Prince. A tiny, one-armed, misshapen old woman sprawls like an amoeba on the Place St. Michel howling in a voice far larger than herself, bitter accusations against the night. What is she saying? The traffic absorbs her words.

She looks like the woman--can this creature be called woman?--we saw years ago in this metro station. There cannot be many who look like her. If she is the same one, then I know her bitter round of a tale almost as well as she does, for it was a howl to sear the memory. She did not rail against the state, the church, or, exactly, her fellow beings. She repeated in a cycle her agony as this: *The fates have wronged me. I am a poor old woman and forgotten. No one cares . The fates have wronged me, I am a poor old woman...* Her fierce, howling mad-dog delivery keeps passersby at their distance. If she begged, she would get what beggars get, a golden nearly worthless pile of twenty-centime pieces flecked with the silver of half-francs and an occasional franc. But she was not begging then and she is not begging now. She is simply broadcasting her bitter lot on this first day of the year.

Luis keeps walking and talking with us, but his head keeps turning back, harkening toward the old amoeba until she is out of sight and hearing.

--Come on, we try to face him forward; he is walking into people.

--I used to live back there, he says, indicating a small parking lot we have just come through. When I first came here, I was living in my car out on the street.

Luis says that he is a man, and that all men are brothers, that we all belong to one another. It is perhaps the Portuguese 'saudade' in his nature that makes him hearken constantly to this idea of brotherhood--saudade being that yearning for something lost now to the world, that the world perhaps has never really had.

...

Today is the day. Today we are leaving Paris, going home. Joel comes back from Nice at four o'clock and crashes for three hours sleep. At eight we're bolting up the Cour du Commerce alley with our baggage, Joel speeding ahead so that when I get to the boulevard St. Germain, he is standing there in triumph, a taxi under his command. He jabbers with the driver and I can just make out his tale of the historic event in Nice this January--snow that has piled up in drifts along the Côte d'Azur beaches. And we had a snowball fight, he says, and our team won! Of course Joel would learn the verb *gagner*, to win.

He sleeps head on my lap for a while on the flight home, and I reflect on all the trouble we have been to each other, which now seems to recede into a forgiving past. I am getting unhappier and unhappier about leaving Robin behind, and Luis and Phillip, and now Joel. I think, I cannot take it. I can't go back to do my hermit act again. Not now.

At the New York airport, Joel finds my car for me, puts me and my bags in it and kisses me goodby. He hands me a note, written on a napkin, saying 'Open it later.' I tell him how nice the island is in January (she's lying) and ask if he won't come visit for a while.

--I've got to go back, Mom, he says with patience. I'm going to school, remember?

I drive in a daze, alone again, arriving at the last minute for the last ferry. I feel so cross, I sit shivering in the bowels of the ship in my car for the entire crossing. On the island, I stop at the A&P for a few things, then drive up the treacherous, icy roads to my lonely house.

I stand inside, looking at the barren rafters, feeling what utter chilly nothingness I am in. No one cherishes solitude more than I, but this is crazy. I think of the warmth and gaiety of the hotel lobby, of Phil there last night singing 'I can't live with you and I can't go on without you.' I see Luis dancing around saying, 'Five hundred dollars, I need just five hundred dollars to go to America. I must go now.' I think of my plan to buy a large suitcase to smuggle the two of them home. They are there now: Phillip making some girl giggle, Luis and Jean Luc planning their next fortune in films.

I think, 'nowhere in the world is there a woman unhappier than I. Just think. Robin is a few hours away in Nice. I'd like to see Nice.'

I think of my friend Bill at home when we were planning a trip together twenty years ago. We plotted with enthusiasm for a couple of hours. Then suddenly he looked crestfallen.

--But why go? said Bill. We would only have to come back in the end.

I never knew what he meant until this moment. Joel's note says, 'Mom: One trip to Europe, for you from me, as soon as I am able.'

For a week I lie in my cabin with a raging sore throat and fever, making phone calls to my elusive landlady and plotting my escape. I can't wait for Joel to make his fortune.

I pack my car and drive the fifteen hundred miles across the treacherous, frozen east, arriving after two dizzying days in Kansas City, where I have no home, at midnight. I call Julie and Hamp, who take me in. Hamp fixes martinis, and at four in the morning we're still dancing to the country music he has put on, 'so you'll know you're home,' Hamp says, 'in Kansas.'

For three weeks I enjoy these dear friends' hospitality, and go out on dates as though I were home from college. I do my taxes, commend my small book business into Julie's care, and fly directly back to Paris.

...

range-sweatered M. Henri reads, intent as ever on his book. At the sound of a suitcase being shoved in the door, he looks up over the top of his glasses and over the top of the reception desk. The sight of me seems in no way to greatly surprise him. In fact, his big, mobile features shift only slightly into an air of comfortable satisfaction. He knew I couldn't stay away.

--Madame Ashmore, he says as though my name were some token I have forgotten. You would like a room.

--Yes, please, I say in my best French. And he says I may have room eleven tonight.

--But tomorrow comes Julie Christie, and then you must move.

--O.K., I say, eyeing him warily and wondering if M. Henri has in these past few weeks lost it.

--It is a nice room, he says smiling, where you may take a nice bath.

I keep looking at M. Henri, trying to decide why he is talking to me like this. Then I remember that rooms with baths are luxuries in small, real French hotels. So he means to be kind, not intrusive about my personal hygiene.

He telephones the floor to find that room eleven is ready, and he gives me a good rate, 'because tomorrow you must move.'

When Phillip shows up beaming in his new persona-- he has a three-day beard and is wearing one of those three-hundred dollar leather jackets that looks like someone found it in the trash--he explains about Julie Christie.

M. Henri was at the desk a few days ago when the telephone rang and a voice saying it was Julie Christie's manager requested a room for her at the hotel.

--*Non* , said M. Henri, a man of culture, a man who knows things, including the literature of France, England, America and Italy and, like all good Parisians, the cinema.

--*Non*, Miss Christie does not stay here. You want the Hotel des Beaux Arts. And he carefully spelled the name and gave the number of the Beaux Arts. Then he hung up.

The phone rang again a few minutes later.

--No, said the manager. It is not the Beaux Arts that she wants. It is the Hotel Saint André des Arts. Your hotel.

M. Henri, alert, unflappable, and generous, replied politely that this was not probable, no not possible. He suggested that the manager check his facts, and requested without rancor as he hung up, that the manager desist.

--Please do not call me again, he said.

The phone rang again immediately and the manager, talking fast, said that Miss Christie had walked by the hotel on her last visit to Paris, looked in, thought it charming, and wanted to stay there. Yes. At the one-star, no-elevator, Hotel Saint André des Arts.

--So, Phillip says, Henri consented at last to give Julie Christie your room.

...

They tell the time of day by her as though she were the sun. A planet in her sphere, it seems, each time I come in I am told with eagerness that I have just missed her.

--But she has just come in, *il y a cinq minutes*, not five minutes ago.

And in the morning when I leave, I am told she has just left, Julie Christie. She has just this minute gone in the car they sent for her, *this big.*

They are not overawed by her; they are like pleased, somber children or a native tribe respectful of natural forces. She is our sun here because she is our nearest star.

Trudging up or tearing down the stairs, even I who will cross the street to avoid seeing a fire or a celebrity, cannot resist, rounding the landing on the second floor, a glance at room eleven.

Often the door is ajar to show a homey splash of light across the foyer's gray, white-polka-dotted wall paper. In a few days, I come to associate the idea of her with that pattern and that light and their intimations that she is in there knitting, rocking by the fire, a cat at her feet, a teapot singing 'time for a little something, then.' Of course there is no fireplace in the room, no rocking chair or teakettle. But I still fully expect to see her, when next I do, with her great mane of white-blonde hair tied back demurely with a gray, white-polka-dotted scarf.

All I have seen of her is the hair and the gray coat as she went up the stairs one day. Unaware that it was she, I watched without particular attention, interested only to see a woman of my age with such a head of hair. And then she turned and tilted her head in the slightest gesture of fatigue, and seemed to sigh, if one can hear a sigh at thirty feet.

No one bothers her, chases after her, demands her autograph. Luis ebulliently declares one day that she favors him.

--She likes me, Julie Christie likes me. Do you see how she smiles at me?

In general there is a festive air, an air of election about the hotel because she has chosen it. She brings the light of her good work that won her her good name. I like to think she notices the respect people show her, and that in leaving her door ajar, her light splashing into the hall, she expresses her trust that here even a star can be a fellow traveler.

--God knows, says Phillip, when I tell him this, they've tried to make her feel at home here. She gets treated just like everybody else--phone calls not taken, or if taken, no message anyone could understand. Some of the reception clerks have never yet looked up at anyone, you know. So they ignore her like they do the rest of us and just start speaking in whatever language they think the person wearing such shoes could never speak. Yes. If she wanted to get away from the goldfish bowl of celebrity, from fawning sycophants, she's found the place.

...

I've slept through breakfast and now am lingering through the lunch hour talking with Luis in the tiny parlor that is the lobby of the hotel and our kitchen table.

--I've got to get some lunch.

--Helen, you must go to the Greek.

--I don't feel like the Greek. I think I'll get some fries from the man around the corner here. And a beer.

--No you will not. He is closed now. You must get a chicken at the market.

--Are they still open?

--Yes, but you must hurry. And some clementines.

--Do you want a chicken? Maybe a falafel would be good. There's so much stuff in it.

--No, not a falafel. No, I have eaten.

--I'll get a beer and half a chicken.

--You must go to Layrac. They have everything.

--Yes, but I don't want everything. Besides they're so expensive.

--You must go. The market is closed now.

--But you said it was open twenty seconds ago.

--Yes. And now it is finished.

A young Malaysian man sits on the window ledge, an anachronistic Buddha in the lotus position against the lace Victorian curtains. He watches us with reserved but open attention, his large dark eyes glistening beneath long black gleaming bangs. I recognize him as the newcomer who beat all the regulars at their Risk game in this room last night. I cheered him on then, and cast a quick smile at him in greeting now. He makes no sign, contributes nothing to the rummaging exchange between Luis and me. But when I start for the door saying *à bientôt* to Luis, he's off the window ledge and standing six feet tall beside me.

--I will come with you. I too must find my lunch.

And so I am surprised to find myself making my way through the Buci market stalls in company with this splendid long-haired exotic creature who tells me he is Mee Kar. Although it is February and snapping cold, and people are huddle-muffled into heavy furs and wools, Mee Kar wears only cotton: black baggies, a big black quilted jacket and thin white cotton socks that come to his ankles: what we call footies.

--Your feet, I say, the international mother.

--I am o.k., says Mee Kar. I usually go barefoot.

He looks all right, that's for sure, striding long-legged and full speed forward like a colt. I cease to worry but not to marvel at him.

We find that while Luis and I have exhausted the conversational possibilities of finding lunch, all the lunch places in the area have closed. We find this at some length, and finally, a mile or two of wandering later, Mee Kar takes charge and guiding me past St. Julien le Pauvre, ushers me into an Indonesian restaurant now empty except for the patron and his family all of whom come over to see to us. Mee Kar seems to know the people and the menu; the food is good and he is good company for one so young and humorless. He tells me he is twenty-two, a makeup artist and hair designer for names even I have heard of--like Dior and Vogue. He exudes creativity, ambition, passion for his work. He instructs me in the machinations of survival in the world of fashion in Paris and Düsseldorf.

As we are finishing our final cup of tea, he looks at me thoughtfully.

--If you like, I will cut your hair, he says.

--I'd like that, I say, smiling at him through my straggling unkempt locks. Then we race back home, avid with purpose.

Luis would like to know where we have been so long, what we have eaten, what we have seen of life out there while he has been chained to his desk. I'm telling him about the soupless noodle soup when I notice that Mee

Kar is no longer beside me. I go out into the hall and see him standing on the first landing, twenty feet up. He clasps his hands and holds them.

--We cut your hair now, yes?

--We cut my hair now yes.

Mee Kar's room holds little that it does not hold when no one is living in it. One well-cut Harris tweed overcoat hangs in the armoire alone. Where are his clothes? He's wearing them.

As he rustles among the riotously colorful tools of his trade--two suitcases full of makeup and hair products--I look through his portfolio. Some of the hairdos are pretty alarming, high and wild with fashion. In the margin by the photos, tiny by 'hair' or 'makeup' is the name Mee Kar.

He sends me to the sink to douse my hair, sits me before the mirror very straight, and starts to cut. I can see from the first clip that he means to do the job and cut my hair.

When I come down for dinner with Suzanne, I'm all in black and pretty close to bald. It is a gorgeous haircut. Everyone says what happened to your hair? And then, 'I like it.'

At dinner, two very sophisticated Berliners are seated next to us and we four talk through dinner together. After, they invite us for drinks and we lead them to the Mazet because, Suzanne says, who's never crossed the threshold of that zoo before, *il faut*. One must, she says, because she is leaving town tomorrow.

The next night we are all singing in our room at about midnight when one of the Berliners shows up, having driven eighty kilometers to visit. I take this to signify that Berliners like short hair and that Mee Kar knows his stuff. People stop me on the street when I go out, asking their way in French. Mee Kar has made me look European, chic. I'm pleased and a little confused.

Phillip really doesn't know. He looks at me in the mirror across our roomful of people.

--Who is that boy? He smiles with something like apology, but like I'm the one who owes it. When I ask him what he really thinks (this is a mistake, isn't it?) he says, I think you should let it grow out. Really long.

I do not like his timing.

--You hate it. So do I, I wail.

But I do not hate it. It is beautiful and good. The lines are perfect. It is so good I feel unworthy of it. Well, it is awfully short.

Mee Kar cuts Phillip's hair and then Joachin's. Phillip does not like his cut although he's ordered every snip along the way and got what he demanded. Joachin's is pretty much shaved off--one blond curl left dangling in his face. Suddenly this shy and handsome cleancut giant looks like he's on designer drugs. None of us likes this look.

Phil grimaces into our crazily ornate Louis Quinz mirror at Joachin's and my sheared heads beside his own.

--Look at us, he says. *The victims of Mee Kar.*

But Mee Kar is my friend. We go out and find food in the markets, bringing it to our rooms to eat together. He leads me around the city to Chinese and Indonesian restaurants where he orders with impressive calm from the page of chicken scratches before my eyes. One night we take a bus and, going through the sparkling lights of the Champs Elysées, we laugh outloud at ourselves, at the privilege, the magic of going out for dinner in the eighth.

One night at a neighborhood Korean restaurant we've been to before, the waiter asks him something in a language that they share and I do not.

--He wants to know if you're my girlfriend, says Mee Kar, deadpan. His Oriental calm strikes me as an admirable trait.

--Tell him I'm your mother.

--We are a funny mother-son. I think no one would believe that story.

Like all my friends in Paris, most of whom are chronological eons younger than I, he has the feeling that I lack direction and that maybe he can help. They are all on track, hard-working and ambitious. To see someone just drifting as I seem to, worries them.

--Perhaps you will come with me and be my secretary when I go back to Düsseldorf, he says. You need something to do.

--This may be true. And thank you for the thought. But I'm afraid I would not be a good secretary.

Mee Kar tells me about the girl he is engaged to, a model. He carries a strip of pictures from a photo booth in the Metro--of a laughing boy and girl, one Oriental and one Caucasian, East meets West. In her model photos, the girl becomes a highbrow woman, fine featured, a sort of mythic princess modeling jewels. We go one day to visit her at Dior, but she cannot get away.

--She is so busy, Mee Kar says, I almost never see her.

On the night of Mardi Gras, when the streets are full of revelers and Luis is out dragging, that is, chasing women, with Phillip, I am standing at the window watching the crowd and feeling sorry for myself and thinking Yeats outloud.

That is no country for old men. The young
In one another's arms, birds in the trees....
Fish, flesh, or fowl, commend all summer long
Whatever is begotten, born, and dies.
Caught in that sensual music all neglect
Monuments of unageing intellect.

Here she is, friends, unageing intellect. Look at that. Are all the men my age in this town lying in doorsteps clutching bottles?

I am moping along these lines when a voice outside my door calls my name in two even syllables: Hel Len, Hel Len. It is Mee Kar.

He has not paid his hotel bill, and M. Philippe has taken his key, leaving him a note that says 'The joke is finish. Pay your bill or you have not room.' This is very strange for this hotel to treat anyone this way. We cannot understand it.

Sharon, the American model Joachin is having an affair with--over Luis's passionate protest that she is a whore and that we must save Joachin from her before it is too late--- has saved Mee Kar, letting him come to her room to make calls to his 'financier' in Düsseldorf. Everyone we know in Paris seems always to be waiting for money, dependent on some guy on another continent who's got the purse strings and a very elusive personal style.

--I've talked to Richard, says Mee Kar. And the money is coming tomorrow. Do you think I could sleep on the floor of your room?

But of course. We clink glasses to celebrate the end of Mee Kar's bad day, and he drinks his wine all at once, like water. Sharon comes to see if I have an iron, which I do not. But I have a shower, which she does not. So we decide to steam her black dress for dinner tonight with some 'important clients.' (I don't know. Maybe Luis is right. More power to her.)

--I am drunk, Mee Kar says dreamily.

And he dissolves into a heap upon the floor to sleep away his troubles to the sound of M. Philippe's water being most flagrantly wasted in the service of fashion.

The next day his money comes and we go over the river and into the big money territory to get it, to have lunch, and, if possible, to see his girl friend. As we make our way through the posh rue du Faubourg St. Honoré, we window shop for clothes that cost ten thousand to a hundred thousand francs.

--I never buy clothes, he says. A friend bought me this.

To me, Mee Kar always looks wonderful--a creature beyond the shriek of fashion and heedless of the herd. I love to walk along beside him, both of us in a sort of absent, cheerful daze, letting the people wonder what this odd couple is, the one so extraordinary and the other so spectacularly not.

One night when a group of ten of us are going out to dinner, he puts his handsome overcoat on me, saying with satisfaction, 'this suits you. This is nice.' He is a faithful friend.

He even does my makeup for me when I go out as a whore. No, no, I mean dressed as one. I can explain.

--Come on, we're going to a party, Phillip says. At Lindsay's.

Lindsay is one of Phillip's California girlfriends. (Unfortunately, I like her, the kiss of death for Phillip's girlfriends; the minute I begin to like one, he drops her to go looking for another.) Lindsay lives on the rue St. Denis with a roommate of relatively blue New England blood. They are students at the Sorbonne, and they are having a party where everyone is to dress in costume as pimps and whores, in honor of the major business of their street.

I watch as everyone gets ready in and out of our room: Toby, our English friend who always looks like 'anyone for tennis?' is got up in a dark turtleneck and dark suit, his hair slicked back, a handsome variation on Brando in 'Guys and Dolls.' Pia, the prettiest Swedish model in the hotel, is gamely wearing a short tight skirt, net hose, extravagant curls and heavy makeup, going as one of the dolls. Luis models at least a dozen different looks before settling for a costume dominated by a Godfather hat that we can't get him to take off for weeks after. Phillip looks fairly like himself, and I am not about to try my luck at this event, when I hear my own voice addressing Mee Kar.

--Would you do my makeup for me if I went?

The next minute I am in Mee Kar's den again, with lamplights trained on my face and Mee Kar a nose away painting my face all over as though I were an Easter egg, expert and very serious. For forty minutes I sit still for this attention while the others come and go with their remarks or silent studies, asking, what are you doing to her? When will she be done?
Finally Mee Kar lets me look. My hair is standing up in stalks. My brows and lids are pink and green. I am, if I may say, quite striking. I grab all the black silk I own and dress in it from the skin out.

--Mee Kar, I say, come with us.

--No, he says. But I feel like a circus act with a trainer.

--Oh, please, please come. (I learned this plea, including the languorous intonation, from Phillip's favorite girlfriend, the lovely, complex Dewi.)

Mee Kar sits silent on the subway while Toby and Pia stand talking. Luis takes a pole in each hand and sedately lowers the Godfather head until he is in a suspended handstand. Phillip plays quietly on the guitar a seat away.

On the rue St. Denis, Mee Kar looks around and says he's made a mistake.

--I did you high class, he says. We did not match the neighborhood.

At the party, the California Sorbonnettes are dressed like Miss Kitty's girls and talking verb inflections. The cheap white wine is flowing. The kids are fun to be with, and sitting on the floor talking something awfully intellectually ambitious with one of the privileged boys, I forget as usual that I'm not one of them.

Mee Kar sits on his haunches in the corner for a while, next to Luis. Both of them look quite serious. Mee Kar is gone within a half an hour. Luis sticks to his post like a statue. When he gets up to get a glass of wine, he has the bad luck to run into me. Inspired by my attire, perhaps, or his, I sail into him, telling him how ridiculous he is with all his posing and chasing women all the time as though it were required--although at just that moment he is more like paralyzed. This scares him half to death, I guess, because his response is this gibberish about my being the most beautiful woman in the room but that he cannot love someone who loves other people he is the one who gets to love others and besides he cannot be tied down. Phillip is right. Luis and I confuse each other. He has one thing right though, right now. I am the *only* woman at the party.

Mee Kar after that evening is really more interested in anyone than me. 'I didn't *do* anything,' I keep thinking. But maybe there is something in Malaysian lore that says if you play a part one time you are forever in it. What could it be? He never is quite the same after that night.

This suits Phillip fine. I was Mee Kar's friend first, but he liked Phillip and adored Luis, as who did not? Luis accepted Mee Kar warmly; Phillip kept him at a distance, fearing the invasion of his life--as long-term hotel residents, to keep sane, quite often do.

But what Phillip really objected to about Mee Kar may have had to do with Risk. The men--the core players were Phillip and Luis, Joachin, and Luis's friend Joseph. They had taken to playing risk in the time that I'd gone to Kansas and come back. They played almost every night.

--Oh, come on. You'll love it. I know that you'll be good, says Phillip.

But after one inattentive evening at the board, I wish never to see the game again, and none of the men particularly wants me to. I just hang around telling them how dumb games are and this one in particular, while they compete earnestly for total domination of the world.

Mee Kar walks in that first night and lets them lure him into their longstanding game. A newcomer! They think they've got one now. This knowing smile goes smugly, surreptitiously around the table. Then Mee Kar just very calmly beats their socks off the first time out. And then again. It's the one night of Risk that I recall with pleasure.

...

It is a good night on the rue St. Andre des Arts. Winter is giving way to light and air. Our windows are open, and we can hear the Arab Beatles singing Simon and Garfunkel as they always do. But tonight they have a crowd, and after every song, applause. We hang out the window to see that their lead singer is back, the one who brings it all together for them. They are not our favorite singers on the street, but we are glad for them tonight and even enjoy them.

Steve, an Englishman who sings American black blues, ambles into our room and picks away quietly on Phil's guitar. Steve has just played a cinema queue, and he reports with casual precision that he and his bottler each made ninety-eight francs. The evidence is growing. Although it's only the end of February, spring is coming to Paris. Life is letting up.

100

And none too soon for Steve, who looked sixty when we met a few weeks ago but now looks about forty-five. Steve is forty-two and getting closer to it all the time.

Mee Kar is in and out of the room constantly, full of the manic energy he's had the past two days. He beams. He bounces, Tigger-like. He springs in like a Jack-in-the-box and makes us jump out of our skins. He will settle down only when he goes back down the hall to his room to work on a project, monklike in concentration, sitting in the lotus position in the middle of the bed, designing hair, designing makeup.

Phillip asks Mee Kar if he knows Kung Fu, and Mee Kar by way of answer pounces into a shimmering stance. Phillip looks at him and finds him too convincing.

--Kung Fu, he says, eyeing Mee Kar warily, is for big muscular guys like you, not big *maigre* guys like me.

And he falls back onto his bed taking his guitar with him. He starts singing his own songs, which I've never heard, and they are terrific. He is shining and tearing it up like a wild man until he is playing the frets with his foot. I look at the clock to see at what time he goes over the edge like this; it is ten o'clock, Robin's manic time.

Jemli, who is working the desk tonight, calls to see where Luis is. Luis is in the shower somewhere, maybe in Mee Kar's room. Jemli says that Paula is waiting for Luis an hour, does he remember that she's here? I say send her up and we will entertain her. Jemli says she is with a friend, with great reservation in his voice as though the friend is something strange, perhaps an elephant. So I say o.k., don't send Paula up.

Phil is in the tub splashing like a kid. When the real Beatles come on the radio singing 'She Loves Me,' I call to him that they sound like us, no wonder they have done so well. And we sing along with it, he splashing in the tub, I on my bed posing as a writer. (I may not have a look, but I do have a pose.)

Luis comes in and says we must go. Steve rises tall and haggardly handsome. Phil, dressing for his gig at the Magnetic Terrace--an expensive club in Les Halles--is extra glamorous tonight. Mee Kar is tall and beautiful. Only Luis is not tall. He is perhaps five ten. But he displaces his space among this forest of tall guys with ease, for Luis is all charm and energy, moving among them with a deft and snappy slide, an athlete among the giraffes. Luis has me thoroughly confused, it is true. Therefore I am typing here in self-defense. He weeps over recordings of the greatest poems in his language. I cannot help admiring him.

He asks me am I coming tonight? I tell him no. He invites me politely. I decline politely. He stands looking at me. He is fascinated by the typewriter. With other men it may be perfume and black lace. With Luis, all it takes is breaking out the typewriter.

--I will come back at two o'clock, he says. And he is gone. I do not know exactly what he means by that. But I do know that he won't be here at two o'clock.

Still, I like him tonight in a way I have not liked him for a long time, what with all we've managed to lather up between us. I like him so much that I am glad it is Paula who is frothing downstairs and I who am singing with Phillip upstairs.

--What? Not coming? But you must come, says Phillip. I always sing better when you're there.

But I can't go tonight. I'm still on last night, when Phil was doing what he does when I come to a show, beaming at every line we've picked out in each song as 'best line'--so that people who do not know that this is how he keeps his act together think I am special to him in some standard way. The beautiful young women in the room look at him, then me, then him.

Last night when two of them came to sit with us during a break, lovely twenty-one-year-olds all dolled up in their Parisian dresses with their Parisian makeup and bracelets and earrings and their charming long hands resting on silk-dressed thighs, Phillip announced to them cheerfully after about five minutes that he and I are room-mates. Confuse and conquer is one of the mottoes around here. Anything but stasis. We share a great fear of boredom, Phillip and I: *ennuiphobia*.

--I'll see you when you come home, I say, a homebody, content.

After he has gone, I sit here happy, pretending to be a writer, listening to the music from the streets and thinking about him at his piano and how he actually has learned to play and plays well, and about what a good night it is tonight on the rue St. André des Arts.

...

The ecstacy of Johann Christian Bach fills the room next morning, and the scene on the street holds me prisoner at my window. Hypnotized by the music, the soft rain, the scene on the jumbled street, I sit watching. All the morning people are hustling by with umbrellas and bags, quiet, through the steady rain, arriving from the Cour du Commerce in the great archway that spills into the rue St. André des Arts exactly across from us. They enter like players on a grand stage, on cue, to perform comic or tragic bit parts.

A clown man in a stocking cap, long hair straggling out, stands skinny in the archway, hands in waistcoat pockets, a bird perched on himself. He stares querulously into a car in the center of the tiny narrow street: who does this person think she is? Others stop to look, but I can only wonder from my window at the Mercedes-gray top and fender. The car pulls off and the clown man stares after it until it is gone. Then so is he.

Girls in big, dark, heavy coats and slacks with hair up in big wheat-sheaves held by big bright plastic barrettes, toss their big bright plastic earrings. They run like fillies in small packs of two or three.

A meticulously attired man with a trim beard and rolled up umbrella rushes into the Mazet as if nothing could slow him on this crucial diplomatic mission.

A few doors down, a small, sad-eyed, middle-aged woman in a trench coat, a russet scarf tied under her chin, stands all compact, hands in pockets by a door she has just tried and failed to open. She is planted there now, knowing, waiting. And in five minutes, they arrive: a dishevelled pudgy woman with the key who enters the door with relief, whose body seems to say, lurching in, 'at last!' A man, too, bedraggled, carries two baskets in behind her--in one a baby, in the other, food and water and wine.

From the arch emerges the star of the morning show: a woman in a beautiful blue coat, wielding an enormous umbrella of wide blue and magenta stripes. She bursts all light and energy onto this gray scene, umbrella first, to stop and look, bright-visaged and intent, not both but all ways. Then with a toss of dark shining hair, she launches herself into flight up the rue St. André borne by her big most beautiful of all umbrellas.

The pinball machine at the Mazet blinks tiny stars beneath the dominance of Amazon Hunter's hulk of flesh. The Mazet people begin drifting in to drift the day away at drinks and talk, and later fights.

A girl of perhaps twenty, with white stockings, black shoes, carefully combed dark, bobbed hair with a pink flower in it, comes into the archway. She stands there center stage, hands in pockets, looking anxiously at the facade of our hotel. She stands just like that for five minutes, as if to say 'Qu'est-ce qu'on va faire?' This cosmic query, literally translated 'what is it that one is going to do?' suggests that there is nothing anyone can do. She looks well-bred and well-confused. She leaves.

In two minutes, she is back. She looks up and down the street from center stage again, leans out, then back, then grasps her hands and pulls herself together. She disappears into the Cour again, her skirt furling around her swift turn. What is it? Why is she so worried? Is she making a ransom-money connection?

A red hat accompanied by a red and black plaid umbrella followed by a red umbrella turn in a splash of color off the street under the arch, into the Cour. A lime-green umbrella moves down this side of the street, reflecting in the window of the Mazet.

The girl appears again, her hand pulling short hair back against her neck. She looks at her watch, arranges something in her purse, pulls her hair into a wave toward her chin, brings her hand to her mouth for a dozen little errands, to touch, to scratch, to smooth the lipstick on, to nibble. She clasps her hands together once again and plants her feet firm, her anchor and her rock. Umbrellas wheel by her face unnoticed.

She turns left into the street this time and walks -- away?-- away. Soon she is back again, tugging her short coat across her neck, chewing her nails, leaning out to look down the street, more anxious than before if possible, as though now it is a question of the bomb that will go off in thirty seconds.

She turns like a toy soldier in a clock from side to side, flicks her fingers, chews them. Finally for a moment, little finger in her mouth, she stands in profile, then begins to work her mouth. All this time her feet are still, demure in flat black shoes placed firm and close together. Once more she stares, dumbly believing, into her watch's face for answers. Now she moves a foot, puts one shoe out and looks at it, brings it back, leans out, almost falling off, pulls on her hair, then steps off the curb into the street and walks off to her right and disappears from sight. She does not come back. One does not know what she is going to do.

•••

W hen I move into an apartment on rue Crébillon up in the Odéon, my first official act is to post a notice on the door: *'Il est formellement interdit jouer au Risk.'* Briefly, 'No Risk.' Mee Kar and Phillip set down the suitcases they've carried from the hotel for me and say nothing about the sign.

Phillip arrives a few hours later with two friends who have come back to town: Tommy, a manic, cherub-faced, blond American who's pushing thirty and looks twenty; and Neil, a black-haired, rosy English lad of twenty in fact dressed in a dark jacket and tie. Tommy is introduced as the best entertainer in the world, Neil as the one all the girls fall for. These billings, which seem excessive, prove in time to be quite accurate.

Tommy sings 'I'll never grow up,' and the three of them are singing 'Cheek to Cheek' when my chic, *très sympa* landlady Nicole walks by and smiles in at us, approving life as the Anglos are approaching it just now. To know them is to love them, we all say. Americans seem generally to think they dislike Parisians; but this is because Americans generally do not know a single one. Nicole, like M. Henri, is ineluctable proof that Parisians can be the most engaging people on the planet.

We make our way to dinner, Phil and Tommy dragging all the girls along the way, Neil staying beside me manfully ignoring them and pressing on. At dinner in a tiny café on rue Quatre Vents, we sit in the muffling warm air of the kitchen, the only room there is, and while Neil describes to me his mum's fool-proof gambling system at the tracks, Tommy opens successively a row of huge steaming pots on the stove and, finding chicken curry in the third, sings to it with great feeling, 'If I had You.'

Tommy eats his meal, then most of everybody else's. He won't sing 'I Won't Dance' with us because Phillip is not drinking.

--It is a crime, says Tommy, not to get as pissed as you can whenever you can.

He invites a pale, lonely stranger to sit with us, and Steven does, saying he is a sailor from Alaska. By the time we leave, Tommy joins Neil and Phillip in singing a farewell to our fellow diners. They applaud and laugh; the owner smiles, flashing white teeth against dark skin and nodding energetically at the parting tribute to 'New York, New York.'

Tommy leads us down the tiny street and into a restaurant full of reserved diners to ask the maître de if they can sing something.

Non! says the man, and follows us into the street to laugh and to exchange rude gestures with Tommy.

We are in a traffic jam in the rue Condé when Tommy grabs Phil's guitar and starts serenading people in their gridlocked cars. 'Oh, she taught me how to yodel, yodel-odellayeehoo...' Irresistible, Tommy has them smiling and applauding from their Renaults and Peugots, no small achievement in this little town. He runs in front of a bus as we try to cross the boulevard, and leaps up and down in front of the great front window, waving wildly, his corkscrew cherub curls bouncing like sprung bedsprings, his green English greatcoat flapping. The bus driver finds him not just resistible but expendable and accelerates as though Tommy were not there. We all fall back and gasp to see Tommy being run down in his prime, mid-bounce. But Tommy, like all good fools and madmen, is not subject to ordinary laws. When we catch up to him, he's in front of the Pub St. Germain giving some German tourists an operatic rendition of 'The Way You Look Tonight.' We go into the Mazet all intact.

Steven is buying drinks for everyone, spending like the sailor that he is. Pretty soon we notice that Tommy isn't there.

--Oh, he's been nicked by the police, says Phillip, who crosses to the hotel to see if Julie's called.

Neil and I are sitting outside the Mazet singing. Or rather Neil is singing and I am singing along sporadically on the parts I know. Three gendarmes, the standard company, come to tell us we must stop. I tell them in French that Neil who's English understands no French. So they tell me in French a lot of things that I don't understand and a couple that I do: namely that it is *interdit* to play after ten o'clock because people are sleeping. Neil tells me when they've gone the arcane rest of what they've said.

--It's all a joke, says Colin, because it is forbidden to play at any time, and no one in Paris is asleep at ten o'clock on Saturday night.

Tommy appears, who's not been nicked at all, but only detained for conversation, the French passion.

--They'll do anything to have a conversation, Tommy says. Even talk to me. But I make them tire of me. They had to talk to me, though, because I was molesting property. Colin was playing the guitar; Colin has an English passport. So they let him go.

--Tommy, says Colin, was playing drums on someone's car, using their windshield wipers as the drumsticks. Tommy was acting crazy, and Tommy is American, so they took him away. I stood right by him. I said 'I've never seen him before in my life. He just came up while I was playing.'

Tommy laughs. It's part of life as a street musician in Paris, where it is *interdit* to play and where on every corner someone is playing. He doesn't care. Today has been a good day for him and Neil and Phillip; they've made over two hundred francs each playing the terraces.

Tommy disappears again as Phil announces that they must practice for the gig tomorrow night. In the hotel lobby, Phil drills us on the harmony to 'Girl Talk' and Neil listens patiently as he corrects repeatedly.

Steven leaves to catch the last metro. He has looked so pale and other worldly when he first came into the café. Now his color is rosy and he looks almost handsome, animated by the energy around him.

--See you tomorrow night, he says. He will show up at Phillip's gig in a surprising new persona, wearing a paisley hat that as Phil says looks like a woman's bikini bottom. He has a kind of dear, direct manner. And even though he buys us all a couple of nights in Paris with his big Alaskan pay, we like him a lot.

I make my way through the Cour du Commerce passage, across the boulevard and home where, before I sleep, I dance in front of the mirror. Nice night, I think as I drift off to sleep on this first night in my new apartment, quite entirely unlike any I would have spent had I stayed home and married my last fiancé in Prairie Village, Kansas.

....

Because I am an iffy cook and usually do not cook at all, Mee Kar and Luis take over on evenings when a lot of people come for a stand-around or sit-on-the-floor or the bed dinner in my luxury studio apartment with its two-burner hotplate.

Bonnie is the youngest of the girls reeled in by Phillip from the hotel and from the metros and movie queues of the neighborhood to come hang out with us on these evenings. They all are beautiful; many of them are models staying at the Hotel St. André, and untrue to the prejudice against the breed, they are intelligent and amiable. But Bonnie is the one that stands out because she has this very strong persona, a sort of edge. She even picks a fight on the first night she comes over, with Neil of all people.

She has the face of the little girl person, freckled and earnest and completely unaffected. But she always dresses head to toe in black. And she has this oddly dark, raspy voice. She loves to joke around, and much of the pleasure of her company is in the gruff innocence of her laughter.

Bonnie is sixteen; she's Danish, and she's five foot ten. I have to look up to Bonnie. Even so, she seems too young to be out here in the world like this alone. She seems this way for about the first five minutes after I meet her. She wants to be a hairdresser, she tells me, but for now she is modeling to make money, as she has done since age thirteen. She has in her career as model been more places than I have heard of. And she has this amazing brash, and it looks like maybe slightly irritating to them way, of instructing the cool Swedish models three and four years her senior, in the way things are on go-sees in Berlin or shoots in Majorca. She monitors their way of dealing with the management at Elite, the agency of most of the girls we know, and makes deft suggestions for improving their professional behavior.

I remember her from that first night because of the way she displaced all the other girls in the room with her vivacity. She sits on the bed giggling with her girlfriend Caroline and they are the essential thing: a film shot of girlfriends sitting on the bed giggling together. Her infectious playfulness takes over me and Dewi, too, when Phillip brings a gorgeous Argentinean bass player over to practice one afternoon a few weeks later, and we perfect ladies demonstrate our appreciation for the finer arts by trying to decide which of the two men has the nicer ass, whispering and giggling, sitting on the bed behind them.

Bonnie and Berthe, her witty Danish model friend who looks like an improvement on Mariel Hemingway, will sit on the bed one night with pen and paper, making out their lists of qualities they want the man they love to have. They do this after I have told them about Carolyn Chute, the author of *The Beans of Egypt Maine*, making a list of the qualities she wants in a man and then going out to find

110

him. He must drive a green (say) pickup and wear a red (say) plaid shirt, have dark hair and a beard. Then, according to my jumbled recollection of this little history, Chute just drives around and checks out the gas stations and pool halls until she finds the man she's looking for and takes him home. Bonnie and Berthe take with high spirits to this notion, and set about to make their lists. Their considerations are somewhat more complicated than those of shirt and pickup colors; they begin with long consultations about what nationality this lucky man should be.

After days of shooting or of go-sees, Bonnie doesn't go back out so often as she calls and says, 'Come to the Relais Odéon and have an omelette with me, o.k.?' And although I dislike the Relais, I readily agree, or tell her to come over and we'll cook.

Bonnie's vibrant courage lives in my memory in that kind of abiding image one cannot capture with a camera. One night she and Berthe and I are having dinner at my place and Bonnie is the cook. She's very late, so we go out to look for her, and sure enough, here she comes up the rue Condé, sort of listing to the right, weighed down by two huge bags full of pasta and onions and bacon and cream and lettuce and clementines. Her full head of blunt-cut dark red hair is bouncing on her shoulder, and every man on the street looks like a predator who'd like a word with her, and she simply does not notice them at all because she knows where she is going--home.

When Bonnie and I go around together, people sometimes ask if we are mother and daughter. I'm proud to have people think this lovely lanky child is mine, irate to be cast in the role of anybody's mother. It is Bonnie's own playful sophistication that delivers us from any standard interpretation of that theme.

She loves to tease Luis, which he fully deserves. He has brought his television to my place, and on Sunday afternoons now, he sits watching the soccer matches in his black muscle shirt, smoking cigarettes while the best sausages and onions sizzle in the kitchen. Bonnie and I walk in on this one day and she says, 'Ugh! Luis how can you stand it?' And she grabs my arm and pulls me right back out the door.

One evening we are drawing on the right side of the brain, she and I, doing pictures upside down from an instruction book. Luis comes in to say that we must stop, that there is a wonderful film about the Titanic on television. So we try to watch with him, but the crazy subtitles for the dialogue make us laugh until we cry, and so we leave.

One day we all leave the apartment at the same time to go over to the hotel, and she pulls me up the street and into a doorway before Luis has a chance to get out the door behind us. When he comes out into the street, he's looking up and down and everywhere. We follow him, dodging behind greatcoats and hiding in doorways when he turns to look. And then we walk into the hotel two minutes after him.

Now this is not adult behavior, which is why I love this child, this woman who becomes after Phillip, my best friend in Paris. I admire her for the way she works so hard. She is a true professional who spends the day being photographed in a bathing suit atop one of the bridges across the Seine, stopping traffic for blocks around, and who at the end of the day does not have much to say about it except, 'Let's go have a salad,' because it is business as usual.

But my favorite image of Bonnie is on a spring Sunday afternoon when we are walking in the Luxembourg gardens. We are paying astute attention to the statues we usually take for granted, of the famous French. We're guessing who they are, giving outrageous reasons, then reading their grave, engraved names and mottoes and laughing at our inspired errors. We notice that no one is playing or even sitting in the grass here. There is in fact very little grass in this gravelly, gray green space. But there is some. And no one's on it.

--What kind of a park is it these French have? cries Bonnie. Just look at all this order. How I hate it! Oh, these French, they cannot let things *be*.

And she tears into a brilliant rage, worthy of Proust's grandmother, against unnatural order.

--They cannot let the flowers grow. Look how they train them, order them around, oh! If you could see the parks in Copenhagen! All green, with grassy rolling hills, plants that are growing everywhere. And forests! And the people everywhere enjoying it. And the Queen comes in a carriage, and the Prince rides a white horse. And each night there are beautiful fireworks. And my friends and I are staying out and having fun all the night. You must see Copenhagen!

....

We are all hanging around the hotel lobby one midnight with Joseph who is working--meaning he's the one who gets up and goes over to the phone when it will not stop ringing, lifts the receiver and puts it back directly.

--While Luis is in Portugal, says Joseph, I will look after you. You must come to dinner with me and my friends on Tuesday.

Luis looks at me darkly as I readily accept, and then at Joseph who smiles and adds--and after we will go to see a film.
When Luis comes back, he wants to know what I have done while he is gone. He teases me about Joseph, whom I have not seen while he is gone, and backs me up against the wall to let me know that he is back. Later I hear him in the shower singing 'Everybody Loves Somebody Some-

time' in this rich, tragicomic Dean Martin voice. I've never heard him sing quite this way before and I am sitting there smiling abstractedly when he rushes in, grabs my hand and tumbles into my stomach kissing it and saying, 'Thank you, madame, for your beauiful body.' Oh Luis.

Spring has come to Paris. We hang out the window singing to the passersby. We walk by the Seine and sit among the tiny greening new leaves on the willow that hangs over us, and in the hazy afternoon I almost go to sleep, dreaming of another river on another new-leafed day, lying with my lover in the sun. Our toes are in the water, tiny fishes nibbling them. Our hearts are full on this our day of days. I come back to present reality and looking at Luis I think of all the ways in which he does not care about me or does not care to show it.

On another evening, I see his intense paleness and the sorrow in his dark eyes and I know that at just that moment we are suffering the dread that comes with love.

He wakes from a dream one day--he never sleeps at night--and says 'I dreamed I was a clone, myself but not myself, you understand. It is my difference from others, I think I do not see the world as other people do.'

Just when I think I'm being my most independent self, he'll see right through me and say, 'I love you, Helen, but not the way you want me to.' He's younger than I, but not so much that it seems appropriate for him to say one day, 'I wish I'd known you when you were thirty years younger.'

--When I was twelve, Luis? Oh listen to this man of thirty-five. And to the men ten or fifteen years older than I who think I'm the perfect age for them.

Miranda, Robin's friend, comes from Nice to visit, and the three of us go to the Rodin museum to find that it is closed. We go shopping then for white slacks for Miranda, and Luis becomes so absorbed in how these slacks fit and these do not that he quite forgets I'm there. And soon I do beg off, as I am prone to do from any shopping tour, and go my way without them. I hate Luis this day for what cannot all be Southern European male machismo, and skulking down the boulevard, scold myself for taking him seriously as a man, an act, I tell myself, of sheerest hostility.

Miranda, our irrepressible art-appreciating and born-to-shop American, calls the next day.

--Well, she says, I knocked off the Louvre this morning and the Rodin museum this afternoon in just thirty minutes!

--Of course she did, says Luis, imperious and glad. Americans have no souls, no appreciation for art, for life. He does not add, for him.

Phillip and I are Luis's friends by special dispensation of this prejudice. Phillip and I are one another's friends by special dispensation of this prejudice because, to a degree, we share it.

Miranda may be quick, but she is thorough in her coverage. She takes me to find the musée Gustave Moreau, the next item on her list. But by the time we get there, it is closing.

--*D'accord, trois minutes*, the guard agrees. And we race in coils up and down and around the spiral staircase through this wild mystical spiritual trip, and tumble out the door again.

--What was that? I say and look into the museum collection catalog I've bought with my last thirty seconds and forty francs.

--We did it in three minutes, says Miranda, smiling.

But we decide not to tell Luis.

'Three minutes,' writes my friend Hoffmann, the art critic back home when I report this art tour to him, 'is just about right for Moreau.'

...

My mother-in-law is coming to visit, my ex-mother in law, that is, but I think of her as present, because except for the fact that Jack and I don't live together, we've kept the family intact in many ways. So, Nadine is coming, and I am thinking of her shining house one night while I look at my own windows and curtains, so that I actually see them. They must be washed. And I must wash them. There's no time for bureaucratic waltzing in *la plus belle langue*.

So I pull up the big overstuffed chair, pile some pillows and telephone books on it, and clambering up this infirm foundation, can almost reach up to their twelve-foot height. I wobble during this operation; but as I coax the curtains off their rod at last, the foundation gives way entirely, and I crash into the windows, breaking one pane. I sit there for a minute, grateful for one thing: I have not tumbled into the street like Edward Bear.

When Luis comes, he gives me his most regretful look and leads me to Samaritan--the Sears of Paris--where with a great deal of confusion about measurements and quality of glass, we finally succeed in buying a pane of glass of the right size and thickness. He seats himself before the broken pane and works patiently away. I cannot believe he's showing such calm competence, and at the work of the working people. I leave the room, hoping the spell will not be broken. But in a few minutes, I hear the crack. After two more trips to Samaritan, the window is as good as new.

--Now, Helen, says Luis, you must not break any more windows. And he stops in front of the great Louis Quinz or Godknowswhich mirror to admire himself for some time.

...

116

March is here and *aller* is the verb to conjugate: he went, she is going, they have gone, we must be going . Everyone always going away now--Suzanne to Crete, Tommy to Spain, Mee Kar to Germany and Toby to England. Dewi and Gia are going to Greece.

Phillip says we must go south, anywhere. To the sun. He doesn't care where. Just south. *Allons-y.* Let's go.

Robin comes up from Nice for a week; we rent a car and on St. Patrick's Day she and Phillip and Neil and I set out to drive her back. Robin wheels bravely through the Paris *arrondissement* traffic and out into a countryside as flat as Kansas. Neil and I split a beer in the back seat and sort out the British vocabulary from the American one for road travel, exchanging our best insults. The Americans gang up on Neil with complaints of the rarefied nature of the entire British vocabulary, for that matter, and he must defend staunchly, finally resorting to that last refuge, 'Whose bloody language is it anyway?'

But we have learned to love American English among these foreign tongues including English, and we are not subdued. We praise its energy and clarity, its honesty and fire. Neil has no one to appeal to, and so must allow our colonial dreams of superiority.

We stop for lunch in a tiny village where, in a tiny, empty restaurant, a woman and a German shepherd come to see to us. The woman carries out the local Rhône wine with platters of cheese and sausages; the dog waits patiently at our feet for the large share he seems to know will fall to him. The bathroom ceiling is five feet high, so we look for dwarfs among the local population. But there are none, and no explanation advances itself except architectural expediency; they did their best with what they had.

Neil drives us through the heavy graying afternoon. It is beginning to snow lightly over the great wide mountains of the valley. Phillip takes one look at the snow and settles into sleep on my lap.

Late in the afternoon, I take the wheel, promptly miss a turn and swerve, skidding into a retaining wall high above the valley with a crash. We get out to see that one of the headlights is broken, and I am so shaken that I'm shaking. Phillip, who is generally made irate by someone's putting him in an awkward situation, takes this life-threatening ineptitude of mine with grace and kindness, consoling me repeatedly, 'It's all right. No one is hurt.' But Neil is glad to get the wheel back again, and we drive into the night singing softly.

We are in the French version of a truck stop at midnight having coffee and *croques monsieur*. Then Robin rides shotgun throughout the night as I seek our way cautiously through the rising jagged red mountains near the coast.

We arrive in Nice in a brilliant pink and gold sunrise over the Côte d'Azur bay. Even our ecstatic carrying on cannot wake Neil, so we leave him sitting upright under his greatcoat fast asleep (he says the oxygen deprivation is the trick to his great gift for sleeping this way) and go into Robin's dormitory.

Her tiny cell has a big window that opens generously upon the spectacular Baie des Anges--Matisse's bay. This makes up for much of the offense of the cement-block rabbit warren architecture of the building complex she and hundreds of her classmates call home at the University of Nice. We sleep until noon, and when we go back to the car for Neil, we find him fast asleep. We pull his coat off his head and call his name. He rolls his head back; his eyes swim up white, and there is just a flash of blue. Then his head drops back onto his chest, his dark curls dangling down his forehead. He is still asleep.

We guide him to Robin's hangout for coffee, where he begins to regain consciousness. Then we go to the beach along the Promenade des Anglais accompanied by a grow-ing crowd of students, Phillip and Neil having as they do a Pied Piper effect.

Phillip goes into the icy water and leaps back to us pounding on his breastbone, shouting 'A chest! I want a chest!' He may be thin, but he is brave--the only one among us or along the long coast as far as we can see who actually swims. Neil, all shining and rested now, works away at his guitar as the girls gather to him.

In the late afternoon, they go for auditions at some local bars in the old town of Nice. They get both gigs immediately. The winter is over for Phillip and Neil.

But I must go back to Paris. So after a week of huddling in the rocks at the beach with Phillip by day and running around to restaurants with him and Neil and Robin and her friends by night, marveling at the beautiful cuisine of Nice, I go. On the night of my birthday I take the night train and am carried like a slab of bacon--or like the Spanish kings piled in their crypts--back to Paris. No one will ever get me on a night train again. They are no place for those who favor light and air and knowledge of the world we live in.

None of the girls in Paris is any too happy with me for taking Neil and Phillip away. And I am not all that pleased myself. But Phillip had kept saying 'I've got to get out of here. I'm going to die if I stay here.' And so it seemed like the least I could do. Too, I was beginning to think my toes could never be warm again, and had a great curiosity to satisfy about them.

Phillip writes from Nice and I am happy to have his news, but lonely without him, without Suzanne, without Tommy, without Mee Kar.

I go into a Weldon Kees funk. Weldon Kees is a San Francisco poet who left his shoes on the Golden Gate bridge in 1955 or so and disappeared, no sign of him again, so no one really knows what happened. But his poem, 'Colloquy' pleases me as the apotheosis, what Joyce might call an epiphany, of a certain human uncertainty. The speaker in 'Colloquy' is feeding the cat.

....I bring, I said, beside this dish of liver and an edge
of cheese, the customary torments,
And the usual wonder why we live
At all, and why the world thins out and perishes
As it has done for me, sieved
As I am toward silences. Where
Are we now? Do we know anything?

I am in full 'where are we now, do we know anything' mode. The uncertainty principle obtains. It occurs to me that causes are not the answer, that a man is not the answer, that answers are not the answer. And what, after all, was the question. Oh, yes. Where are we now, do we know anything?

My French is so uncertain that I find myself, instead of speaking to shopkeepers and neighbors, making pleasant sounds by way of greeting and goodbye. The sounds beneath a language--the raw material of which the words are made--are distinctive. Anyone can tell the sheer sound of a German from that of an Italian an Englishman or an American, without one articulated word. And I am pretty good at making the French sounds even if I can't get the articles or the verbs much less the sentence structure right.

One Sunday in May I find myself threading my way through the tall buildings of the sixth, searching for sunlight and standing on corners where I find it, plotting how to find it next. I am just stumbling around Paris making these sounds and searching for the sun and wondering why I choose to live this way.

I think about my fear and loathing of prevailing Noah's Ark standards, of how something in the human spirit dies, cannot survive in that scenario at all. I want a life, one that can be distinguished from others as my own. That's what I am doing here. This is just part of the hard part, the days like this full of doubt and fear. The trial. As the macho guys on the surfboards sailing full force straight into the rocks say in the cartoon, 'This is the part I hate.'

But I embrace the pain along with the possibilities, and I know that I must make mistakes and that I want them to be my own. I do not want a lifestyle according to the contemporary gospel of magazine articles. I want a life, to be life-sized. I want life that has a human core from the first syllable of recorded time. Therefore this odyssey, this I can't go on, I'll go on.

Thinking of the trials of the human spirit, I recall one of the most difficult evenings in my Paris memory, one spent at a disco in the Bastille in the dead of winter.

I was really in no mood, but Ellen had invited me to a nightclub with dinner chez Madeleine first, and I had agreed to go. In the afternoon I wandered over to see Jim Haynes at the Village Voice, but even his southern charm and his nuzzling my neck while I looked through a book of William Burroughs essays did nothing more than give me a little false hit. I felt like my friend, another Jim, years ago when we were tossing down last drinks at Kelly's bar in Kansas City, getting ready to pile into Ted's Ferrari and go to a Rudolph Serkin concert.

--*Damn* these pleasures, Jim had said. *I want happiness.*

Ellen said it was all right to bring Phillip along to dinner at Madeleine's first. But Ellen always says it is all right to bring people along to other people's parties. And it seemed that Madeleine had not been reached and therefore did not know that we were on our way.

--Oh well. It is too late now, I say to Phillip. If it's a big cocktail party, we can just slither through the buffet line and disappear into the crowd.

--It will be all right, he assures me, although he does not look as though he thinks so himself.

I lose a two-hundred franc note on the way over, and Phillip drags me into an all black all male bar where he dashes off in search of Kleenex while I sit there with my irises until his head pops up again, a white bobbing buoy in a sea of black. He is desperate for a Kleenex.

--There's not a stick of paper in this whole place, he says through his nasal block. Not a napkin, not a scrap of toilet paper. How do they do it?

We find Ellen on the street and walk together up three long flights, admiring the broad carved bannister. We knock, listening for party noises. A shining matronly woman greets us and we enter Madeleine's elegant apartment, leading with the irises and champagne.

But they are not enough to make up for the fact that the table is set for four. We are crashing a dinner party for four people.

--Well, Phillip hisses back at me, they need us. Four is not enough.

I am trying to back out the door, hoping Madeleine will think she imagined she saw another woman. But Stephan and Daphne, her children, come to sit and talk with the adults. Daphne has a friend staying the night. I am floored at the grace with which all three teenagers greet us. In my country, we would speak of their astonishing social skills, but that cold, tinny phrase communicates nothing of the warmth and humanity these beautiful children and their mother give to us, their uninvited guests.

Stephan who has just had his first lesson in classical guitar, plays a small melody. Daphne and her friend kiss us each sweetly twice on both cheeks and go off to another room to giggle.

The other dinner guests arrive: Sidi and Marie-France. She is about thirty, white and dressed in all white. Sidi seems ageless, all ages and no age, a man. The name he goes by means, simply, 'sir' in his native tongue. He is Senegalese, dressed rather fantastically; perhaps this is a traditional celebratory costume. Marie-France is reserved to the point of seeming unfriendly. Sidi is eager and smiling and impersonal. He has the air of the professional entertainer which tonight he is. We are to go later to hear his group play at a nightclub in Bastille.

Dinner is amusing, thanks in part to my mistaking the first course of sausages and rice for the entire meal. Even the looks Phillip and Ellen give me as I help myself to a demure third round of it do not stop me. By the main course of course I cannot eat. There is a lot of wine and champagne, and the conversation turns on little linguistic vagaries and spirals off so that soon none of us has a clear idea of what we are talking about or in which language.

After dinner, Stephan brings the guitar for the musicians and asks them to play. Phillip plays and sings an intense new French ballad at the height of popularity in Paris, and the girls come running from their room to sing with him. Then he and I sing the one country song he admits into his world, 'Seems like I can't live with you.'

When Sidi takes the guitar, he is concentrating, meditating, drawing on some cultural, timeless depth that seems downright competitive. But it is hypnotic, and from my trance, I feel a sort of embarrassment for me and Phillip that we are so rootless. I do not know if Phillip feels this, and we do not speak of it. But after dinner, he accompanies us to the metro stop, then abruptly excuses himself and leaves.

As we stand on the train lurching from poles like rubber balls on rubber bands on wooden paddles, Ellen scolds me for not bringing Phillip up better.

--It is not my job to tell him what to do, I say. He is an adult.

--You must be a Marine sergeant with men like Phillip, Ellen says. Get tough. Stop making excuses for him.

But I have let Phillip go his own way, so it is me and Ellen and Madeleine and Marie and Sidi appropriately in his harem clothes: a ruffled ivory silk shirt and red balloon pants. He is spangled and bejeweled beyond imagination, but his white turban tops him off with an air of monastic simplicity.

The Bastille neighborhood is rough, the walk from the metro a little edgy, but no one really bothers to do much more than stare at Sidi and his all-white harem.

The foyer of the bar is grim and gray. A locked steel door blocks entry. There is a cover charge no one seems to have anticipated. The steel door is opened long enough for Sidi and Marie to go through. The door is locked again in our faces and we are told that we must wait ten minutes. I would pay a handsome sum to be let out of here instead of in.

The ads have said ten o'clock. It is almost eleven. At eleven they allow us along with the others who have gathered in this sullen interim, into a long room, along a long bar and into a dance floor surrounded by two- and four-person booths and low tables with just lower benches. The room is empty, but all tables except for the ones behind pillars have reserved signs. A man comes to tell us that we must put our coats in the *vestiaire* and pay five dollars each for the privilege. We refuse. He insists. Only when we say we will leave does he leave us alone. But he does not bother us about our coats again. Drinks are five and six dollars each, also obligatory. We settle onto a plastic bench with ethnic fabric seat covers.

Recorded Afro-disco music blasts the dim lit room: a 'They Shoot Horses, Don't They' mirrored ball splats spots of light across us and the now six other people in the room, all men. For an hour the music blares as the crowd trickles in: a blonde white woman with two black men; a white man and a black man; two white girls, a white couple, five white boys, two black men.

It takes a while before I realize what is missing here. It is any black woman in any configuration. Later, when the crowd has gathered to a crush so that the dance floor is solid with bodies, not one of them is that of a black woman. I register this observation with Ellen who says it is their own fault if they do not come. No one is making them stay home. Their isolation is self-imposed.

But I am in the grip of an idea: that something is wrong here. Just what it is and what it means I cannot tell. I know the white woman black man thing is considered chic among some Parisians. But that is not enough to explain the total absence in a public place of this size and character, of black female persons.

I am about as out of sorts as I can be, studying which circle in the Inferno this most nearly corresponds to, and watching Marie-France dance alone, the only dancer in the center of the huge room while the Afro-disco piped in music blares. I notice that her black low-heeled pumps are awfully bourgeois for this scene, and am told by way of explanation that she is a sociologist and the daughter of a director at Dior. She met Sidi in Senegal and they have been together for several years. Sidi was Madeleine's lover for a while, and things got rocky for the three-way friendship, but that is all over now. This is a more than adequate answer to many implications of my impertinent question. But it does not in my mind explain the conservative black pumps.

Marie sits down. Sidi comes from his conversation in a booth across the way, beams on her, hugs her.

A black man with a long pony tail, a baseball cap, a white shirt, tight red leather pants and boots comes to greet us. He is the leader of the band; he welcomes us smiling and saying things I cannot hear over the music. But I am grateful for the feeling he conveys, and the hostility I feel in this place, in me, lets up a little.

One by one people get up as though moved by the spirit at an evangelical camp meeting, and dance. They dance solo and cool to the recorded sounds. The black lights are on now-- all white glows brilliant, iridescent in the shapes of pants and shirts and collars that appear to have lives of their own.

A girl in white jeans and t-shirt is a glowing column in black light. Marie's white dress does not glow, but the big round buttons down the front of it do, and the one just around the back on her hip. She knows where she is and what she is doing. I do not like her any better for it.

Ellen goes to dance, then Madeleine, like large earth mothers graceful and statuesque among the wiry, fiery other dancers. I watch a dancer in black with short, stiff hair, sleeves rolled like a truck driver's t-shirt with cigarettes at the shoulder. Ellen insists that she is a girl; Madeleine and I say boy. But of course that is the last thing that seems to matter here, now.

There is no couple dancing. Everyone continues to orbit solo, connecting only in a hint of tribal ritual or shared space. Boys and girls and men and women ignore one another so completely that there is an absence of the predatory feeling one gets in American clubs. The sexuality is here, but generalized, diffuse.

And as for dress, everyone looks dressed for the fire --as though they've grabbed from the chair beside the bed the quickest costume that can be assembled running downstairs bent for leather. The regulation costume is worn jeans and rumpled sweaters. Nothing chic or blatantly expensive. To be dressed in the sense that one dresses to go out is the one dress-code proscription here, clearly. My black silk dress, appropriate for teas and funerals in the midwest, could not feel more ridiculous. If I'd just left my nightgown on, I'd feel a lot more comfortable.

The crowd of solo dancers all seem to have pretty much the same subtle this-year's moves. But one black guy in a black t-shirt with a green abstract pattern on it--after Marie the longest dance-floor resident this evening--is moving in increasingly energetic and complicated patterns, as though achieving a great improvisational jazz solo. He ups the ante for the crowd; dancers around him pick up on his more frenetic and complicated energy.

A pretty young woman enters with a grey-haired man and joins us. I am made somehow to understand above the deafening music that she is a doctor. She kisses us all and sits down. After a minute, she takes off her sweater and sits there like a Maidenform ad in a little silk and lace camisole top and jeans. Meanwhile her older man takes Madeleine to the floor to dance and Madeleine gives a little squeal of delight as they go. But couple dancing does not become the evening's trend.

It is getting really hot. People on the dance floor are ripping off sweaters and jackets with desperate efficiency, not missing a step. A group of five boys comes to sit near us; the one by me tries to talk to me, but I cannot hear his words. He gets up and goes to the dance floor and hangs around it eyeing the crowd with this tough-guy look. But then the spirit has him and--who woulda thought?--he enters the crowd dancing slightly, almost delicately. When the music lets up he comes back and asks for a light.

The band comes on, a regulation drummer, two other percussionists on bongo and congo drums, two guitarists, the man in the red pants on an instrument that looks like a hybrid xylophone-drum, and three singer-dancers: Sidi and two women, one white and one mulatto. The sound level is so high that I cannot hear without putting my fingers in my ears.

The dance floor crowd gathers in a semicircle like Big Band fans in forties films. The first song is about police cars and fire trucks, I guess. It is extravagantly noisy and filled with sounds from Paris streets. The drummer is incredibly *on*, and with the others forms a sort of percussionist Supersax. Superstix, maybe. I admire them but cannot stand them.

How can these people take this deafening noise? It occurs to me that maybe they are all deaf. Or perhaps they are so drugged out that this is what it takes to reach them. Aren't they afraid of going deaf, then? No, they don't look it. Do they fear anything? The French press shows the most blase'attitude toward AIDS, so I think it may be true that they fear nothing, not deafness, not lethal disease.

'I am out of my league here,' I think, watching the steady intense pitch-black drummer who holds back nothing of himself while I sit here in my tea dress with my fingers in my ears.

I can't take it, I somehow communicate to Ellen. As she and Madeleine walk me out, I make a last check for any black woman in the place. No. Not a one. Unless you count the very light mulatto singer.

Out on the street, I search in vain for a taxi, then push through a motorcycle gang at the Bastille metro to catch the last train out. I am too exhausted to think about running through metro corridors trying to make train connections and avoid weirdos at one o'clock, so I take the stop I recognize as closest to home on this line, and walk from the Hôtel de Ville.

Using Notre Dame as a star to guide me, I find that it is long enough and cold enough, but not really an unpleasant walk except for the tension I feel in my shoulders and my face. I keep up a nonstop lecture to myself saying, 'cool it who do you think you are what are you so worried about this is Paris you are in the world what did you think that it would be like it is a nice evening enjoy it look at that the Hotel de Ville at night the Notre Dame get with it woman.'

This lecture running through my brain, I cut through the shishkabob alley and into the Place St. Michel where I am assaulted by a rash of 'bon soir *madames* and bon soir *mademoiselles*,' and all I can think is *these bastards cannot even tell the women from the girls.*

I am so glad to be out of the long metro corridors that I almost do not care, thinking that soon I'll be away from the least charming charm of Paris, these preying men.

And when I turn into the rue St. André des Arts I realize how sweet and civilized this street is compared to those I've come from. It is like a country lane with birds and flowers to my battered sensibilities. Footfalls echo soft and clear off the close old buildings that line the street. I know I am glad to be here because even the Mazet looks like home and mother to me, chicken soup and apple pie. I do not go in, but I am glad to see it.

I go directly to my room and shut the door behind me thinking this is your basic nightmare educational evening. I could have done without it. But boy am I glad to be here. And boy does Phillip know what he is doing. Marine sergeant, my eye. I am going to ask him to raise me to have more sense.

The next day I call Ellen to say not exactly thank you but how much do I owe you, and don't be mad at me.

--Don't be mad at *me*, she says.

--I'm not, I say. But I will say this about those black women wherever they are. They're awfully smart.

...

That

would be waving and that would be crying,
Crying and shouting and meaning farewell,
Farewell in the eyes and farewell at the centre,
Just to stand still without moving a hand.

---Wallace Stevens, *Waving Adieu, Adieu, Adieu*

I come home from dinner with Dewi and Gia one night quite late and the phone is ringing, ringing. I can hear it as I come up the steps, unlock the door. It is Luis. He must come over now, he says. I am about to ask what is the matter but he hangs up.

A few minutes later, he is at the door. I open it and he sweeps by me breathless and pale green--that sort of iridescent color he turns when he is upset.

--My mother was right! he says with terror in his eye.

Something in his tone makes me think his mother has chosen this rather late moment to tell him the truth about women.

--Helen. She is here. In Paris. With the baby.

--Your mother has a baby?

--Isabelle. She is here. In Paris. With the baby.

He seizes his television, his radio, some clothes, his France Soirs and Pariscopes and Tele 7 Jours, the emblems of the not *haut* side of his cultural passions.

--I'll call you. I'll bring her to see you, yes? I'll call.

And he is gone. The next day I pack the rest of his things, thinking of the order in which they came in on that glacial natural force that erodes the distance between two bodies. First the toothbrush and the t-shirts, then the radio and pots and pans, the television and a growing wardrobe in the closet. I think how glad I am to see the television go.

But I will miss Luis. In spite of probably because of his erratic passions, his loyal treachery. No more will he arrive in the morning after working at the hotel all night, carrying the hot fresh croissants of early morning Paris and calling my name as though he has not seen me in a year.

I take his things to the hotel to be rid of him and them and to get on with it. My lease here is up in a few weeks, and I am going back to the states. Fair is fair. But yet.

As I approach the hotel through the Cour du Commerce carrying bags of Luis's things, I see a woman I've never seen come out the door and turn up the street. I think 'I've seen her somewhere. She looks kind of like me.'

Of course! It is the pregnant laughing woman in the photo, Isabelle. And of course she is my type. Proust has told us and told us that a man falls in love with the same woman over and over again, in many women all of one definite type. The nagging question is, how much of Proust's erotic wisdom obtains in heterosexual affairs?

--It is worker's day, says Luis when he calls on the fifth of May. And no one in Paris is working except me.

--Toby is there, he says.

--Toby is where?

--He is there.

--Toby's not here, I say, looking around the room.

--Yes. He is here. In Paris. At the hotel. Now. I have just seen him.

--Oh. You mean Toby is there.

--Yes. That is what I said. Toby is there.

Oh, I am going to miss Luis.

...

The last night I saw Mee Kar he arrived quite late--for he is shy about occasions where one is expected to have fun. And on my luxurious two-burner hot plate, he followed Luis's first course of chicken and vegetables with his second course of rice and omelettes for the fourteen of us jammed into my room. We said we'd talk the next day about his renting my apartment while I was gone to Greece. The next day, Luis was sleeping when I went out in the afternoon, and I took the phone off the hook before I left. When I called the day after, they told me he had gone. I telephoned Phillip.

--He's gone, he said. And he was quite upset with you. Said something about how he was supposed to take your apartment and that you hadn't called. He left for the Gare du Nord an hour ago.

I ran down to the Metro and, arriving at the Gare du Nord twenty minutes later, combed the crowd for tall Malaysians all in baggy black. I ran along the tracks feeling like the heroine in a thirties' black and white film, searching the faces in the windows of the trains going to Germany. I looked for Mee Kar for an hour, looking in all sorts of useless concourses. And then I just sat there feeling rotten.

If I could change one gesture from those two years, it would be that I would not take the phone off the hook on that May day in Paris. It seemed to me symbolic of our fragility, of the whole experience of being out there in the world alone as we all were, where friends are strangers and the life we shared was made of moments quickened by their sheer unlikeliness. I made a false move, complicated no doubt by some cross-cultural confusion, and let a friend down. It really angered me that I opted for Luis's comfort--Luis who had me right at the very middle of his priorities while Mee Kar did what he said he'd do, down to the minute.

But there it is, that nagging regret, right now as strong as it was when I was searching faces in train windows in the gigantic hopeless Gare du Nord. Mee Kar wherever you are, I am sorry. Please call home.

...

Dewi and Gia, who are studying at La Varenne, stage an Easter dinner that alone could justify their fathers' hundred-dollar-a-day output for tuition at that last word cooking school. When Bonnie and Berthe and I are finding our way back from their Île St. Louis apartment after, we look up at the windows of the Coq d'Or and call out, 'Eat your hearts out, people, we have just had a meal that puts yours to shame.'

--Oh, do come to Greece with us, say Dewi and Gia. The sun, the beach, the sea, the life--it will be wonderful.

I am telling Toby, who is back in town now, about the Greek plan at lunch one day, and he and I get up from our booth at the Pub St. Germain and go around the corner to the travel agency that knows us all so well, to see about some tickets. Toby says 'what, tomorrow?' So he's out. But next thing we're standing in line at the change bank and Toby introduces me to his friend Hugh, a Canadian comedy writer who never cracks a smile, and Hugh says he is looking for a place to stay.

I rent Hugh my apartment for three weeks; he brings his stuff over, pays the rent; we go out to dinner with Toby, and at midnight Hugh puts me in a taxi on the Boulevard St. Germain.

In two hours I'm on the plane for Athens, my fist full of Hugh's money that has made this sojourn possible.

In Athens, I check out the ferry schedule to the islands. I am to meet Dewi and Gia in Mykonos tomorrow, but the first ferry goes to Crete. So I call them and explain. The first ferry goes to Crete. They understand. It is a twelve-hour ride, overnight. I like the idea that I may find Suzanne.

The steward who carries my bags to the room asks if I am English.

--No, American.

--You are South American?

--No, North American.

--You are not American?

--I am American.

--You are traveling with your husband?

--No.

--Ah, then. I will come for you tonight after nine.

--No, thank you.

--Yes. We will drink coffee and we will talk.

--No, we will not.

Greek men, somebody says, treat unescorted woman like whores. It doesn't feel like that exactly. More like he thinks I am free game. I try to decide if there is any chance that I am being sullen and he is simply being hospitable. I thank him once again and ask him for my keys.

--There are no keys, he says. And he goes off, refusing my tip.

I am too tired to worry that I've offended him or if he is going to walk through my no key room and jump me in the night. I have some wine with dinner and sleep straight through the night in the gently rocking arms of the Aegean.

...

--You are English? says Katrina, a lanky, vibrant green-eyed Greek of maybe thirty who reminds me of Melina Mercouri and who has my arm in hers and is walking me along the beach of the beautiful roaring Mediterranean in the tiny town of Ierapetra on Crete.

Ierapetra says one of my guidebooks, the southernmost town in Europe, is not a tourist town. It is not recommended. Could anything make me happier to be here?

I've gotten off the bus and walked to one of the little cafés by the sea for breakfast. The owner has answered my question about local accommodations by telephoning Katrina. And Katrina has walked up five minutes later, brimming with the joy of life, to say, 'Yes. Come to my hotel.'

--You are Italian? Katrina guesses again.

--No, I am American. My name is Helen.

--American! she cries. You are American! And you have the great Greek name, Elena! She hugs my arm.

Up the stairs of Katrina's clean hotel we go and, gesturing at a smiling old woman in black who is mopping the second landing, Katrina by way of explanation and introduction, says 'Mama, Elena! Elena, Mama! '

Mama, square and beaming, repeats my name and as I pass smiling, pats me on the back.

My top-floor room is huge and beautiful and sparkling clean, all full of sea air, and it seems the sea itself would come in but for a retaining wall that has been built about one hundred feet from the row of buildings the hotel is on. The sea crashes against the wall, leaping fifty feet into the air, and it is hard to believe that the sea puts up with the wall at all. Only the race with Odysseus in it would try to get by with this trick on nature.

I ask the price. A double with a bathroom, its going rate says Katrina is ten dollars, but I must have it for seven. I cannot argue. After Katrina leaves, I slide the glass doors open and breathing in the brilliant seascape, I think 'Paris. Paris! I do not care if I never see it again.'

I've entered Iraklion harbor on the north coast of Crete at seven this morning in a fog worthy of the one Aeneas wraps himself in to enter Dido's court. But the fog has lifted its deceptions to reveal the striking, savage sea coast of this island country, and I have not been able to stop myself from thinking how this stark grandeur would strike dead the kind of sentimental blather Martha's Vineyard can inspire. This beauty forbids trivialization; there will be no Hallmark treatment here. Even my lovely Maroc orange brought from the Buci market, looks puny and ridiculous beside the giant Greek orange I am given for my breakfast by the tumultuous sea.

In the afternoon, a storm is blowing in, the roar increasing, the green deepening. Part of a broken boat is washing in. Its forward rush and dip and disappearance, then springing into sight again, recalls Juno's rage in action in the *Anead*.

Men hung on crests; to some a yawning trough
Uncovered bottom, boiling waves and sand.

The storm increases until I begin to feel that I have come here to die a violent and untimely death. I think it will be good to die in such a place, and to do so with dignity. I sit in a café by the sea, unusually attentive to the passing world.

The next day, I am thrown against the bottom of the sea by a great wave, and fighting my way up furiously and losing out and realizing I may not get out of this at all, I think my intuition is quite keen and that my family and friends will say, but what was she doing *there*?

I realize there is no way to find Suzanne here, so I mail her a postcard, and the next day, returning from the beach I find her note in my door. I'll find her, it says, along the row of cafés where I am staying. Mornings, she says, she sits with her coffee by the sea, writing a novel. What? A novel by the sea? And what has happened to the research from the Bibliothèque Nationale?

She comes around the corner out of the old Turkish quarter where she lives, and we walk right into one another. She is tanned and vivid in all white--a transformation from her Paris look. She wore the same thing in Paris every day: a black blouse and a drab green skirt. Actually there were two black shirts, alike. I admired the principle to distraction, but found the particulars, especially the second same shirt, distracting. Here she is beautiful in the way that one could only intuit in Paris. Here she leads a life among friends and neighbors, fishermen and businessmen--a life I am privileged to admire and even share up to but not including disco dancing.

After ten days of eating, sleeping, talking, singing and drinking by the sea--I even danced a few times, but that is not natural to me and somehow doesn't seem to count-- I take the boat to Santorini for a week on that bright white rejuvenating island, and then I'm on a plane again, Athens to Paris. When I come up from the Luxembourg Garden metro and see the lamplight glowing on the lovely trees, I think, how dear my neighborhood, how sweet to be here in this magic place again. Robin and her French boyfriend Philippe are waiting for me in my apartment, which makes the feeling whole. I am glad to be at home again in Paris and sorry that I leave again so soon.

...

B onnie and Phillip and I pad through the all quiet Luxembourg Gardens early on the soft gray last day of May. They are helping carry my baggage-- and isn't *that* the right word--into the dawn of my departure for the United States. I don't know why I'm going. I'm going because I am going.

They jump the turnstiles at the deserted Luxembourg station, while I protest loudly and Bonnie says with a wave of her hand in her knowing way that it is a holiday and that none of the metro police are ever about on holidays. Everything goes according to her prediction for miles and miles. But about thirty minutes out, as we near Orly, the train stops at a suburban station, and a dozen metro squad police swarm on. We have seen these guys in action and know to fear them. It has not been long since I saw them beat a young black man bloody on this very line.

We grab the bags and jump out. The train with its swarm of metro flics pulls away.

Phillip looks over the eight-foot wall that runs along the tracks; he spots a pâtisserie bustling with early morning business. We can smell the bread. He jumps the wall in a second and runs toward the shop. Bonnie and I stand there for a few minutes trying to decide what to do.

--Buy tickets, I think.

--Yes, tickets. But we just stand there.

When the next train comes, I get on, wrestling my bags on with me in a test to see if I can do it. It is not a graceful sight. Bonnie races down to buy tickets.

Phillip's head appears over the top of the wall, then the rest of him, and he reaches out and hands me an apricot tart through the train window. He looks distressed--maybe because he is eight feet up over a train track and in a tenuous state legally as well--but he just scrunches up his handsome face and says, 'don't go.'

Bonnie comes back with the tickets to get them back to Paris legally and stands on the platform on the other side not waving or saying anything.

--Write, says Phillip, who knows I will. But none of us seems to know what to say to punctuate the end of the conversation that has made us glad for months.

Bonnie somehow says it best: goodbye in the eyes and goodbye at the center, just standing still without moving a hand.

I didn't know about a Wallace Stevens goodbye until I read his poem in the winter in the woods of West Tisbury months later. But I knew the minute I read it that Bonnie at age sixteen knew more about saying goodbye than anyone I have ever known.

...

The walkway retracts the minute we sit down on the plane for London; there is hardly time to contemplate the likelihood of the man in front of me being psychotic before the pilot announces takeoff. How very 'let's go!' he sounds. I am stunned to think we are really going to take off on time. I've never been on a flight that took off on time--that is, actually, to the minute, on time before, so I am absorbed in the miracle of this new experience.

I only absently contemplate the man in front of me until I see that this man is plainly weird. Yes, maybe psychotic. His features including his ears--are ears features?--and eyes and nose are small, like he is made of beads and buttons. His head is practically shaved, his complexion unhealthy mottled white as though he's been living in the pipes under the city for the last few years. Beneath his black leather jacket he wears a stark white t-shirt.

The engines are roaring. We really are going to take off. We are taxiing. But here comes another guy to speak to the psychotic. This one looks like a mountain boy from another century. He has a large head and large features. He is swarthy, oak-haired, young. He wears heavy definitely foreign boots, gray cotton flannel pants cut like long underwear, and a heavy eighty-percent gray sweater. They exchange fierce whispers in a foreign tongue, and finally the young one seems to have the message. He goes into the bathroom.

I am certain now that we are going to be hijacked. But that is ordinary; I am much more impressed that we are going to be hijacked in a plane that took off *on time*, and I plan to mention that to the press when we are interviewed after the ordeal. Should I survive, of course. I am hoping to survive if only to bear witness to this historic fact.

Time passes. The plane idles. The stewardess walks to the back of the plane to chat with the bathroom door. We cannot take off with him in there. After several minutes and several more conversations through the door, he emerges and she escorts him to the seat nearest the bathroom. This rugged boy looks ashen now, with dark circles under his eyes. She sits with him like a mother, and we take off ten minutes behind schedule as he bends double holding his legs.

We rise through the dense underwater gray of early Paris morning, going gray into the clouds and --boom!--we break the water line into bright blue sky with feathery clouds. Below, a snowbound brilliant landscape bursts into sight--the unspeakable magnificent topography of the clouds. Some days the lay of the cloud land could be Wyoming or Colorado, but today it is pretty Kansas--large flat stretches with patterned rivulets like flocked wallpaper in Johnson County, the kind that would be called in the sample books 'Regency.'

The hour-long trip from Paris is a glorious show, and I want to applaud as we land in London--incidentally without incident, thanks no doubt to the rugged mountain radical's weak stomach.

...

A sign saying 'Watch Your Clothes' hangs above the series of belt walkways that convey passengers from the waiting areas to the departure gates at Gatwick. I've been watching the clothes, and they are the thing to watch.

The airport is teeming with big, beautiful black persons all dressed for the great public pageant here as saints or angels. Their fanciful full-length costumes must be at risk of catching in the conveyor belts. Therefore the official 'Watch Your Clothes.'

One especially splendid man in a sky-blue robe lightning streaked with silver white and more white embroidered in great swirls at the shoulders and hem, with a cap of the same cloth to top him fabulously off, lifts his skirts delicately as he steps onto the belt to be carried away apparently to heaven.

He is not royal or sacred I am told, but Nigerian, and the Nigerians are the great traditional dressers. Yet the handsome friendly and sophisticated woman across from me is also Nigerian and her dress appears to have come from some fashionable house this season. And who am I to even try to note this, wearing my jeans as usual?

A recurring toot-toot announces motorized carts of citizens driving through the airport crowd. We walkers and sitters look at them closely as they roll close by us, to determine the nature of their privilege. Age alone seems to merit a ride, or crutches of course. But the robust, rotund and regal black couple splendid in silver and golden robes and hats, seem to have their privilege by birthright. 'Must be the Queen of Sheba,' laughs a man with an American accent, louder than he needs to, so that I am humiliated for my country. But even he seems rather more pleased than irked at the truly splendid sight, for it is one of the privileges of the traveler to behold the world in all its pomp and circumstance.

As the plane rises from LaGuardia at sunset, the horizon of night meets that of day. The wide stripe of night in the east bends like a blue-black rug up a red wall that glows into bands of bright orange to pale orange to yellow-white to the vast blue promise of daylight where we are headed, west.

Manhattan below is a map of itself laid out in infinite points of light. Lines sparkle and swirl in dotted curved planes of yellow, blue, green, red and white lights. This is it: the conceptual art project to end all art projects: Inherit the earth. Give it roads and bridges and cities and light them into magic by night.

How can anyone not want a window seat on this amazing spectacle? How puny Christo and his flapping plastic fences and sidewalks and freezer-bag wrapped bridges are by comparison, although there is of course no comparison.

...

J ack comes up from Houston, and on a brilliant, scorching, true July day we drive from Kansas City to Lawrence, Kansas and buy a tidy white house in a deep green flowering yard. The house is in the shadow of the 'hill' as the University of Kansas campus is called. The house will be a home for Robin and Joel while they are in school; it will be storage for my books and furniture and for me when I need, as I do now, to catch my financial and emotional breath.

But most of all we think of it as a little family home. Guilt, no doubt, lots of guilt. But, too, we have had an amicable divorce, a phenomenon virtually unheard of at the time. Now, twelve years later, we are buying a house to help keep our family close. Maybe this will become a trend, too, we say. People can escape the Noah's Ark condition of traditional marriage yet keep a place that they can call their own in the world.

We drive back to Kansas City along the old highway by the Kaw River, one rarely used to eat up the thirty-eight miles between Kansas City and Lawrence, for it is poky with tractors to slow you to an attentive crawl through the scenic lowlands known hereabouts inelegantly as the bottoms.

We sometimes took this drive on Sundays when we were first married and living in Lawrence. We muse on the philosophy of home. 'Home,' says Warren in the Death of the Hired Man, 'is a place where, when you have to go there, they have to take you in.' And Mary replies, 'I should have called it something you somehow haven't to deserve.' Acknowledging that Warren has his point, we side with Mary.

In any case, there will be no more worrying about Joel's being on the street when the dorms close for Thanksgiving. And it will give us all a place to land when we come to visit old friends and family in Kansas City. We can meet here for family blowouts on birthdays and such, we say. We are right about all of this; the year will unfold to a richness of family gatherings in the kitchen of the little house featuring a variety of far-flung friends and relations.

Jack and I sit in the Pizza Hut in Lawrence between the time we first see the house and an hour later when we sign the papers for it, and work out the financial and personal details of this venture. We decide to tell Robin and Joel that neither has to live there, that either can leave it with the other who in turn can bring in a friend to pay rent. Such rent in turn will go to the sibling living elsewhere. The big bedroom gets my bed and books; the rule for it is that they can use it as they like but that when I come they have to let me in.

When Robin returns from France and we tell her she has a house with a brother and sometimes a mother in it, she is not ecstatic. But she isn't checking out either. As student housing goes, our little vinyl house is luxury accommodations. So Robin and Joel move in there together, uncannily resembling Jack and me twenty years ago. Robin yells at Joel for leaving his socks on the stove; Joel, dauntless and loving, tells her to fuck off.

This arrangement pleases Jack and me enormously, maybe because it gives us a family focal point again. Or maybe it is just revenge: let them be the domestic homebodies and worry about the plumbing and the gas bills for a while.

But for whatever reason, as we drive along the river in the brilliant day hazy with familiar Kansas summer heat and dust, we feel golden and happy. It is as if we somehow still have a hold on the promise we held when we were young. The difference is of course that then we didn't know we had it. Now we know not only what we had but what we have.

--We should get married again, says Jack, who loves a bad joke. Just to fool them.

--And destroy our happy family? Don't be frivolous, dear. We've worked too hard for this.

Jack goes back to his life in Houston, and I settle into the little house with my books, piano, scrapbooks and children for August in Kansas.

I am sitting at my desk one day when I realize that it is a perfect day in Lawrence, Kansas. The sky is empire blue and opulent with white comforter clouds. The air comes in light and cool on the breeze that waltzes these sweet frail old-lady curtains around my window on the world. Here, today, Vermont Street.

Just minutes ago the men from the Kansas Power and Light tree-trimming service dragged the felled and leafy branches from our grand old midwestern back yard elms down the driveway and into the street where they fed them to Olathe Chipper, a rackety, ravenous animal machine that ate them up and spewed them into the back of the truck. The last I saw of Olathe Chipper, he was trailing along dutifully behind his mother truck, quietly confident that he was rolling toward his next meal.

Now the street is quiet in the way that big, old, small-town streets are quiet--perfectly. An occasional child or bearded Lawrence grown-up--almost certainly a university student or teacher--pedals by. A dog barks once, is still for a moment, then barks again, once. It is a rare August day that is perfect in Kansas, but this one is.

I have been cleaning out the garage of our new house, sweeping the rafters and walls, fussing under built-ins and around work-table legs, choking and wondering when the last compulsive bourgeois batted a broom around the place.

A penny found on the work table suggests that the last husband to putter here did so fourteen years ago. Another penny found on the floor in a corner hints that the compulsive collector of miscellaneous lumber, broomsticks and curtain rods stood these sticks here in a corner bin some twenty-six years ago. 'Someday they'll come in handy,' he thought. Someday maybe they will.

I like these men for their avocation of puttering in the garage, for the bolts and sticks of lumber they saved. One was passionate for window shades and curtain rods, sold

146

them perhaps. There are dozens here, some still carefully wrapped and marked: new, if the word can be used for matter so brittle and so long rolled tight in its ways.

In the same corner with the twenty-six-year-old penny, what looks like an old leatherette cushion for a child's chair turns over to reveal four wheels. Belly-up like this, it identifies itself as a Kitchen Kreeper. "Saves Labor, Saves Knees, Speeds Work," and available from the Kitchen Kreeper Company of Ashtabula, Ohio. A graphic shows an aproned woman on her knees on the thing accompanied by a bucket on its twin.

The picture suggests that a woman on a Kitchen Kreeper could locomote around the kitchen floor washing and scrubbing swift as a swallow. I try it out and find it a bit rusty and slow. I feel funny on my knees there; somewhat as I imagine I might feel if someone were to come up the drive and find me here naked. I am not only in the servile position, I am in the presenting position.

I get up dusting off my knees and wondering if any good woman ever lost it on one of these things and, suffering a lucid moment of full comprehension of her circumstances, got on her Kreeper and sailed through the house describing crazy circles before crashing into the closet for a landing, packing her bag and getting out.

I look at the woman in the graphic here and doubt that she ever did that. I have in the past few days seen this woman many times, and I have been thinking about her. She is featured in pictures in the owners' manuals for all our newly acquired old appliances.

The refrigerator, the stove, the washer--every one is a twenty-to-thirty-year-old paragon of delightful design, a triumph of the industrial imagination. And there she is, that woman, with every one. And she is the apotheosis of what seems to be a complete failure of imagination.

The appliances are informed with the spirit of a world from which the woman seems de facto to be barred. The refrigerator light, an incandescent blue swirl around the lyric GE logo, hints at interplanetary ritual. A similar light on the stove can sweep me away at twilight with its neon promise of galactic travel. Even the Mediterranean azure of the washer tub suggests a sort of Bermuda Triangle into which I could tumble free of gravity, into another dimension.

But the Woman of the Owners' Manuals, that woman--with her neutral smiling face, her sensible short haircut with its modest waves, her house dress, her arms full of laundry or her hands plying pots and pans and milk cartons--she seems to have no possibility of any other function than the work she is doing now. She hints at no future, not even her own. Especially not her own.

She projects no hint of motion, no more than that of the dog on the chain: no travel here or there or anywhere, on or off the planet.

She is of course the unvarying present, the worker of the work that is always there and always to be done. She is every owner man's dream: stasis made manifest in an aproned, patient, smiling wife and mother. Her charm is habit: predictability, repetition, being there on the treadmill powered by the chaos that is daily life. Her job is order, a house tamed to approximate the grave of the happy dead.

Where is that woman now, I wonder. And I recognize that she is still right here. Part of me is that woman. True, part of me wanted the New York Times this morning and biked down to get it, and part of me is eager to be free again in the great world. But that woman in me is happy to be here, in this present, in this role. I am content beyond description to be here in a house with my children, a house with a history of puttering husbands and patient wives.

I am honored to be fixing dinner on a stove that wants to fly to the moon, standing barefoot on linoleum as the incredible sweetness of the summer day wafts through the screen door from the deep back yard where bright flowers bloom and vegetables ripen in sunlight just beyond the giant sheltering elms.

The part of me that is that woman is happy on a brilliant, perfect summer day in a small town in Kansas where just now on Vermont street the ice cream man comes ringing by and two small children fly from their houses, singing sweet names as screen doors bang jubilantly in their wake.

...

Services! The word rings with the promise of easy big bucks. It is to the eighties what plastics was to the era of 'The Graduate.' In cities from New York to Tokyo greedy elves are plotting in hotel basements to deliver a bottle of scotch to the unwary traveler for seventy-five dollars American or to return your laundered undershirt with a bill for eleven-fifty, to bring on the caterers to feed your forty guests for only fifty dollars a head. More than half the work force in our own self-reliant country, we are told, now earns its greed--excuse me, its bread--from services.

But services are not the thing yet in Lawrence. In Lawrence we are still on Emerson. In Lawrence, the word is self-reliance and you are expected to be able to do things for yourself.

When I am home for Christmas in the little house, I call Art, who has inspected the house in August when we bought it, to chat with him about the matter of the pipes which it seems are frozen.

Does Art remember the house? The little one on Vermont? Yes, Art says, he does. And the thing to do now about the freezing pipes is this. Go to the store and get some heat tape and some insulating tape. Wrap the heat tape around the pipes about once a foot, he says, and then wrap the insulating tape over it. Nothing to it.

But the pipes are in a crawl space, an unpleasant place at any time of year, especially inhospitable in deep December. Hesitantly, therefore, I ask if Art himself ever undertakes such projects or knows a plumber who might be willing to. But Art is ready for me.

--Most people, he says, just do that themselves.

So I dress out and throw myself onto my knees in the foot deep snow to see what's going on in the crawl space. As I squint into the morass from a window-well, I see what looks like an eight-hundred square foot swimming pool. Water is standing a foot deep in there.

Do I call Art and whine? I do not. I call the local rental people and ask them what most people do when their houses are moored over a foot of Kansas rainfall, now turning into an ice rink for short persons.

--You just come on out here, honey, says Marcie at Jones' Rentals, and we'll get you fixed right up.

So I do and they do and I put the sump pump in the basement and drain it for two days. My nephew Bruce shows up, a Christmas miracle, to do some of the slogging dirty work. And Marcie gives me the pump for a second day free because the water's not gone yet and because it's Christmas.

--It'll be your Christmas present, she says merrily.

Joy to the World. But I am embarrassed to show up in Lawrence only long enough to try to sheet my block over with ice. The quality of life on Vermont Street is not right now generally enhanced by our gift to the street: everything out there is covered with ice from our house: the sidewalk, the street, for a telltale hundred yards. But we don't have to concentrate on hiding from the neighbors. At this time of year, everyone just runs from the house to the car without looking right or left.

And besides, if they do figure out what's going on here, they'll have to admire me by local convention. If I am not doing much for the neighborhood otherwise, I am showing that I am a credit to it in this way: I am doing what most people do in Lawrence and being self-reliant.

When I go to have my coat looked at, Dolores at The Shop-- for that is all they call it: The Shop--looks at it for quite a while, her blond curls bouncing in a row above the glasses perched on her nose. Then she looks at me.

--You'll have to treat it, she says over the top of the glasses.

--Treat it?

--Yes. You'll have to go up to George's and get some oil and treat it. First you use the oil, then you use a balm. Furriers do it. But you can do it yourself. Then I'll see what we can do with it.

--What furriers? Is there one in town.

--Well, no, I think you'll have to go to the city for that.

--Could you treat it for me?

--Oh no, you'll have to do that.

--How long does it take?

--Oh, weeks, I think. I don't really know. It was Chuck--he used to be here and he did all the furs, I don't do furs myself--who always told people to go to George's. And it seems to me it was quite a process--a couple of weeks for this, a couple of weeks for that, and then you wait a couple of weeks and do something else.

So I go to George's where a nice woman in a bad mood because she is not supposed to have to work that day tells me she doesn't have any idea what I'm talking about, I'll have to talk to Doris, George's wife. George is out of town.

Doris gives me Chuck's phone number and I call Chuck who is as nice as he can be and confident of my ability to mend my coat.

--Oh, sure you can do it. Anyplace carries the oil, like K-Mart even. Then you need some cheesecloth-like tape, but you can't get it here. You'll have to get it from a furrier.

I check with every furrier in Kansas City but no one wants to let me in on the cheesecloth tape. So I call Chuck again to ask if he can just cut the coat down for me.

--I'll look at it and see, says Chuck. And then to my delight he adds the words that tell me I've sounded the limits of self-reliance in Lawrence.

--Of course you could do it yourself, he says, but that probably wouldn't be a very good idea.

...

R obin bounds in from Ulitmate practice fixed on a
fix. She eats cookie dough with her fingers, adding
chocolate and peanut butter to it as she goes. It is
not a pretty sight. But I am not going to worry about
Robin. She is bright and beautiful and good way out of
normal range.

--Wash your hands?

--Uhmm.

--Did you?

--Yes, Mom.

--I can remember eating whole packages of cookies and
what are those things with peanut butter and chocolate,
of those anyway, when I was in my twenties. I think
you get over the worst of it at about thirty if I
remember right. You ought to eat some protein.

She sits down to have some salad while she waits for
the cookies to bake.

--Put some chicken in.

--Ugh, that smells awful.

--Oh. Well, don't put it in. Listen. There's a
grasshopper about this big out on the window sill in
the back room. I went out there and saw him and said
whoa, buddy, and he said 'don't mess with me or I'll
spit tobacco juice all over you.' So I left him alone. But
he's out there. Big.

--Mom. I think you're bored.

--Bored? I'm not bored.

--Remember when you told me you thought I was deeply and seriously bored?

--Uhhum.

--Well I think that's the way you are now. You're made happy by the littlest things.

--You mean I'm being a disgusting old person, yammering on about the most trivial things. I'm boring. But I'm not bored. You were dragging around the house, wouldn't talk, didn't show any interest in anything. I know I'm weird, but I'm not bored. Being made happy by small things is something I've learned. Anyway, you're going to scream bloody murder when you see the grasshopper, knowing you.

I leave Robin to eat in peace and go to my room as Pascal has told us all to do, dear friends, if we truly desire any good in the world. I think of riding the bus on Crete, going from Iraklion to Ierapetra trying to read the signs in Greek until it came to me that that was a profoundly obtuse effort. 'Things are the sons of heaven, and words are the daughters of men,' Doctor Samuel Johnson says, with unnecessary sexism it is true but his 18th century point is taken: that words, the names of things are secondary, dependent creatures while things themselves are the strength and the reality of the world. Things are meant to be perceived in other ways than by naming. Naming is not only not enough, it is no way to understand things.

I hear Luis reproaching me for my limited ability to see and smell, taste and touch, for my overexercised intellect. I rebuke myself with, 'There is more in responding to the world than naming, classifying and judging, although you couldn't tell it by *your* behavior sometimes. I answer bravely, 'I am willing to change. I'd like to learn other avenues to perception.'

154

I go back to talking to Robin silently while she chomps alfalfa sprouts in the kitchen unawares. 'I know it is not your world view that one can be happy in the way I am. But I am. And it keeps gaining on me. I feel like the Last Duchess--all things please me. I thought I was happier than I'd ever been on the island last fall. And then I was ecstatic living in the middle of Paris with you and Joel in room thirty-two. Then in Paris alone I felt the challenge as a pleasure too. I am learning to love the world I used to fear. Including the grasshoppers. Maybe you're right. Maybe I am bored.'

...

I hate to be unpleasant about my home town, but many of us are, and it is on my mind just down the road here. The thing is not to get wired on the subject.

I loved this home town for forty years so that no matter what glamorous cities gave me place and work, I always longed for its auto-rhythm and always fled back to its comfortable arms, to the habit, the *petit train-train* that was my life in Kansas City.

I am not ungrateful to Kansas City. It has given me a glad heart. It has taught me that if I can't say anything nice, I mustn't say anything at all. I'll say this: but for Kansas City, I could not be so grateful for West Tisbury and Paris and Lawrence, Kansas. Or for Sam Beckett.

Maybe it is predictable that where my oldest, dearest friends and most of my family are, I manage to have almost no life that could in any way be distinguished as my own rather than somebody else's.

But there is something in the town itself. People who come here and like it always talk about how comfortable Kansas City is. And this is true. Its stifling conservatism and concrete power structure render citizens blissfully comatose to what might be called life. (Maybe this is overstated. I don't know. I can hear them now. They're *very proud* of Kansas City and its culture. And its trees and fountains. But speaking for myself, the time came when I felt quite dead there and after that a few years, buried.)

Most of my energy when I'm in the territory goes into staying metaphorically anyway in my room, and physically out of parts of Johnson County, Kansas, a place where important Kansas City people dwell protected from what city life there is. This Kansas suburb of the Missouri Kansas City was the scene of my last stand in this territory.

Kansas City, Kansas is a disspirited but real and ethnically rich town in Wyandotte County. Johnson County's classy cousins are places like Chevy Chase, Maryland and Upper Arlington, Ohio. But Johnson County itself could happen only on the Great Plains, in the Wild West, in the Bible Belt.

I lived, after I sold the Kansas City (Missouri) house, near the corner of Mission Road and Eighty-third street in Johnson County. It is this corner and the memory of it that strikes a note of fear deep in my psyche. Not of my own apartment, a quiet, pleasant, quirky place with a distinctly assorted company of neighbors, but of the shopping center across the street called Corinth Square and dominated by an acre-sized supermarket called straightforwardly and deceitfully Payless. This Payless and its attendant boutiques comprise for me the outward and visible signs of the inward and spiritual condition of Johnson County.

The store itself, a gigantic sprawl of wall-to-wall carpeting with Muzak oozing over every inch, has the genteel elan of a funeral parlor and caters to women in Talbot classics or pastel velour jogging suits appropriate to conquering its miles of track.

I am loyal to my kind, and yet when these pertly coiffed and carefully made-up Johnson County women get into their Lincolns and Mercedeses out on the asphalt plain that is the Payless parking lot, they create from their own celebrated nurturing and sharing female nature what is indisputably the me-first capital of the world.

They get in, rev up, and without looking back at all, gun it gloriously into each others' shining fenders. I've watched this going on for years, and my conclusion is that each believes sincerely in her good woman's heart, that there is no question of right of way here, because there are no other rights than hers.

It is to me one of the most spiritually perilous and aesthetically terrifying places in the world, perhaps itself alone sufficient reason for leaving home and, once finding the sanity and grace of Alley's porch, refusing to go back.

...

I've loved being in Lawrence, and have been able to do research in the library here that makes working in the celebrated 42nd street library in New York seem like Dante working in prison compared, that is if Dante had had to research the *Commedia* which he did not, having the body of knowledge of his time in the library that was his own free head.

But now it is time to go again. And like Alexander campaigning into India, I determine to burn my baggage. Fire and ice, my offerings to Lawrence. Well, maybe instead of a parting bonfire, I'll try to sell these things.

I run three ads in the Lawrence paper: for the car (Auto), the typewriter (Business Equipment), and for some furniture and clothes (Moving). They cost twenty-seven dollars and somehow I know I'll never see it again.

But I almost enjoy the work of getting ready for the sale: frantic, compulsive, do-everything-at-once work during which I get to change my mind at least twenty times a minute. My kind.

I run errands and fill the tank to cure this unappealing aspect of a gas gauge needle lying poverty-stricken on 'E.' I hear sounds in I've never heard before, sounds of the end, the clutch going, the transmission falling to the ground. But it's too late to think about that now.

A run to the bookseller is my last errand, to see what I can get for ten big books.

--Three dollars, says the woman at the desk.

--That's mean, I say. I ask her what she will get for the Barthes reader alone.

--Ten, she says.

Maybe it is the fact that I've reviewed four of the five big hardbacks she is holding that makes me resent this devaluation so. I thank her elaborately for her trouble and hugging my literature shove my way back out the door. If Alexander had behaved this stupidly, he never would have made the Khyber Pass.

The sale hours announced in my ad are eleven to seven, which seems reasonable for an early September Sunday in a college town. I remember that the Lawrence newspaper is one of the few afternoon papers left in the world. I take a nap.

At two, I go into the garage to price things. It must be over one hundred degrees. So I come back and read until four at which time a lady knocks at the back door and asks if the sale is over. I say I hope it isn't and she asks about the Mission Oak chairs. I say they are big. She says she needs a chair for her nephew who is studying law and who moves around all the time when he studies, from his room to the kitchen, all over. I say these chairs are essentially immovable. She likes them and asks how much. When I tell her she says she is sure they are worth it but she doesn't want to pay that much. I say that they probably wouldn't suit a peripatetic philosopher like her nephew, and she asks what's in the garage.

She noses around some things, asks about the shoes, picks up a red pair, says they are nice but too small for her and besides she can't wear low heels because she has high arches and must wear high heels or no heels but low heels hurt her feet. Her feet look to me smaller than the red shoes, but of course that is no longer the issue in this complex denouement.

I walk into the cooler air outside the garage. She looks around the dresses and boys' shirts a bit longer, then turns and calls out to me.

--Do you have anything for men to sing in? Like velvet?'

I have to say that I do not.

She asks about the car, says it is pretty but that her husband requires an automatic shift because he can't see very well and he gets around just fine considering, but...

I say it really is a boy's car I don't know what I'm doing with it, but she wants to know how many miles it has, how many miles it gets to the gallon, how many cylinders it has. I know the answers to the first questions, and guess the last one is six; it's been a long time since I've heard much talk about eight-cylinder engines, since the days of my father's Buicks. I had a Buick, too, but that is much later and it only had six. I don't fill her in on my cylinder history however, because she is telling me about a man from Lawrence who has moved to the Vineyard if only she can think of his name I should try to find him when I go back because he loves to talk to anybody from Lawrence. I am eager to hear his name because although I am not sure I an enough from Lawrence to count, it would be nice to have another person to talk to if I try to make it through the winter on the island. But she doesn't remember his name. She introduces herself as my down-the-street neighbor.

Looking back at the garage, she says, aren't books expensive and our bookseller here won't give us anything for them I can't believe how much my husband spends there. I am interested to know what kind of books he buys but she is looking at the car again, saying how nice it is. When she leaves, I think maybe someday I'll meet her in the grocery where it will seem natural and possible over the radishes and watermelons to ask who she knows that sings in velvet and what he sings.

A bearded blonde man comes running up breathless and asks if the cherry chest is gone. He explains that he and his wife have a waterbed but that waterbed furniture basically is not very nice but they've found a beautiful four-poster cherry bed frame and fallen in love with it and have been looking everywhere for a cherry chest. All the furniture people keep telling him the same thing, 'No. No cherry. Nope. Nobody buys cherry around here now.' But he likes cherry and so we stand there admiring the cherry chest for some time.

I say he can have it for seventy five dollars because the drawer is chipped and the mirror gone. He pulls out his check book saying as he does so that he has no checks and adding, as a sort of bonus *non sequitur*, that his wife has told him it was the last check when he left. He asks if I will hold it for him anyway and he'll come back but probably not later this evening because he and his wife are sitting for the neighbors' three children along with their own three. I say morning will be good.

He walks back to hold up the deep pink, deeply flounced and gathered frou-frou curtains that were in Robin's room when we bought the house. (No way, she said.) He asks how many there are and is pleased because three is just the number of windows in their bedroom. And he stands there smiling behind this great pink cloud of a scarf so that I can not help thinking of Sally Rand.

They'd be nice with the four-poster he says and I agree saying they are pretty but unacceptable to my daughter who is into stark right now, black and white, that sort of thing. He says he'll be back, you just can't find a cherry wood chest in this area anymore and you can't even get close to a new one for seven hundred dollars. I say I'll try to get the mirror back from my sometime husband who has removed it to Houston while I was in Paris.

Nothing is simple these days, in the public or the private market.

--I'll be back in the morning, he says, but probably late in the morning because I'm a pastor.

I nod and smile a little stupidly I think and watch his blond stocky person in retreat wondering what flock he pastors on Monday mornings. I am not about to ask. I hope he comes back for the cherry chest, though. It seems that whatever gods there are have arranged this.

Two girls come by, Native Americans, with a troop of three handsome boys of about eight.

--Got any toys? asks one of the boys.

I don't and say so feeling genuinely sorry, but one of the women says thank you so somberly and quickly that then I am glad I don't.

I want to ask about Indian life in Lawrence and consider remarking on the Haskell football game, for I've heard shouts from the stadium of our local Native American college the night before.

But it doesn't seem that it is going to come out right, the three of us women trying to talk about a football game, and maybe they hate football anyway. I certainly don't like it and don't want to talk about it. I can't, however, go directly to the subject I am interested in, with some opener like, 'You're Indian, aren't you? I've been noticing the Indians in Lawrence this time as I did not when I was a student here, and I often admire their full-bodied, earthy grace as they walk quietly in twos and threes in the dusty evenings along the streets of town, even the busiest streets, unhurried, while us major culture dumbbells thunder by in our bullying, smelly cars.'

No occasion for this line of rambling arrives. So I must content myself with admiring first the fact that although they are small women, their large breasts won't fit into the tailored jackets and snug-cut blouses that fit the overeducated women in this family. (I read some article asserting a connection long ago and have yet to free my mind of it. Is there *any* assertion that has not been made somewhere in a magazine article?) And I get to admire their frugal sensible choices.One buys the four-slice toaster for three dollars, and four place settings of pottery for five.

The other buys two India-Indian embroidered gauze shirts; the luscious deep magenta one has been Robin's favorite at one time and it pleases me to see it going on to another life.

I accept a check for eight dollars and they leave. The sale is over.

I put two dollars cash in my pocket, turn out the lights, lock the garage door, and go for a walk in Lawrence, a town where people paid at the turn of the century the most loving attention to detail and variety in their architecture.

The breeze is fall cool, the night sounds summer warm, and as I walk I calculate that at my present rate I will have paid off the cost of the ads--easy--by this time tomorrow. Maybe one of the books will sell.

Thinking about my advertised 'heavy-duty professional never-down' typewriter that has not sold and is not likely to at the reasonable yet astronomical asking price, I dutifully report to it, uncertain of who owns whom around here anyway.

When I leave Lawrence it is by car, my car, with my big typewriter smugly in the back seat still in possession of me, and with the full awareness that it needs a sharper will than mine to be an Alexander.

...

arrellin

across I-70, still itself, I'm in my ususal state of state of on-the-road exaltation. The cattle grazing around dish receivers as big as barns appear to me to be attracted by the promise of high-tech careers. The beloved haybales are out in force, although the haybales going east from Kansas City are nothing to the ones on the road west.

Old highway 40 runs along beside I-70 in different color tones, as though it is taken from a different movie reel. The reel features a bunch of shabby haybales standing around with old refrigerators and junked cars by a small house tucked in a hollow, like cousins drinking beer at a Sunday reunion. Seedy though the particulars, the scene recalls the rustic light and yearning charm of Constable.

A Jesus sign superimposed over a hamburger stand sign greets drivers at dusk with the good news of an upcoming JESUS BURGER KING. An ADULT BOOKS sign blares neon pink over a truck stop motel in a stretch of dark open Indiana plain, suggesting a rather low moment in flatland culture.

From the looks of things at the DariQueen this Friday night, there's not much to do in Terre Haute but eat, so that unless you are genetically incapable of doing so, you get pretty fat. Two skinny teen queens with bluejeans like Toreador pants and hairdos like permanented and lacquered top hats are working against their odds right now.

The place is jam packed and the kids are whirling like dervishes to get the Queenburgers and Darifries out of the bins and onto the counter for this horde of impatient overweights. Cars are lined up for two blocks at the drive-in window, and through blaring static the yearnings of the carbound are announced.

Into the crush inside, like riders into a subway at rush hour, charge forty subteenagers, herded through the doors by three determined chaperones. A pretty worker, serene as a mountain lake, is explaining to the two teen queens the nature of the 89c Butter Pecan Sundae, its weight and height and what the choices are besides whipped cream and nuts. She doesn't look at all chagrined when, totally oblivious to the two-hundred anxious addicts surging behind them, they ask, next, about the Chocolate Delight. One of those sweet women who show up in the most unexpected contexts, the madonna of the Terre Haute D-Q.

The adults whine in a self-conscience demonstration of subservience to children and pay an elaborate and doting attention that the choosing of an ice cream does not require.

The kids wear different brands of tennis shoes and even other kinds of shoes. There's clearly no agreed- upon, must-have fashion in any of their clothes. It is astounding, like finding the last frontier.

The adults however and many of the children wear puffy nylon coats; the teacher who seems to wield the most status has a quilted knee-length fashion over wide flare-legged pants. It looks as if the way to fashion status here is via the ever fatter coat.

Large moms and dads clench numbered tickets in their fists and stare intently at the coral counter while the children wriggle across from them in coral plastic booths.

A group of girls all giggles clatter into the booths they stake as territory with their rambunctious racket. They are still giggling and gossiping in my ears over the singing of my tires east on I-70 again.

At a Howard Johnson's on the Pennsylvania turnpike, a boy and girl about sixteen are sitting in the next booth talking quietly. His voice rises as he says, well you're *not* going to see him any more.

--Why not?

--Because that's the way I want it and that's the way it's going to be.

--But we're only friends. And what about Heidi?

166

--Who I see is my business, not yours. That's a completely different thing.

--Heidi is going to be a whore anyway, but what you do with her is your decision. I don't see why you have to do everything for her you do for me.

--I don't.

--Yes you do.

--No I don't.

--Did you give us the same bracelet for Christmas?

--I told you. What I do is my business.

Ah, young love in the Stone Age. Can these things still be going on? How sweet it is to be eating and drinking and going off to sleep--against such a foil as this--alone.

God knows I've played my own ludicrous scenes with men, and not without some pleasure. Interestingly, the big attachment, the one affair I got into since leaving home that is by any definition real or possible has no grip whatever on my imagination and therefore can't be recounted except in barest outline. It was of that breathless sort: meeting as strangers on a stretch of deserted beach in winter, letters each day, flowers every weekend, plans for forever; in short, romance. Then I remembered what the whole thing was all about: domesticity and Noah's Ark, being in the same cage with the same creature for the duration, and I weaseled out of it. I noticed belatedly but yet in time that this man did not read interesting books, though any excuse would have done. By this time the beloved himself had observed that my domestication quotient was below par and he was not himself too sorry to get out of it. As for my assimilation of the experience of

167

this narrow escape from bondage, I've repressed it I guess, because it largely escapes my recollection. I do know that Stephen divorced his wife and called me and I that it had been so long I couldn't remember what he was talking about. I did have the grace (or knee-jerk reflex) to admit some guilt, of which my friend Kate cured me immediately with the line, 'Oh don't worry about Stephen. A man like that. Some other woman will snap him up in a minute.'

Anyway, I say all this because when I got back to the island, I got into an unlikely scenario even for me. He was fifteen years younger than I, probably functionally illiterate, and my relationship with him while sexual was in no way libidinous. So there is no reason to remember him so well except that he was of a generous and adventurous nature--by no means a domestic or domesticating creature--in short, a man who had my attention as I had his: for a while.

When I think of him, I think, boy, when we have the big Mr. Wrong Contest International, I'm going to have a competitive entry, but then again I think of another friend Kate picking up one of her lovers at the county jail for their first date, and of Barbara who went off in a VW bus with this maniac who had an M-16, and I think I may not actually have a hands-down winner after all.

...

Whenever I try to think about how I came to be with a man like that, as it would be intoned by my family if they ever got wind of it which they will not because I never tell them anything, because I do not want to hear that extended snivelling that translates, 'Oh, why won't you find a nice man who is right for you?'--as if I haven't had enough nice men who are right for me, though I never can stay with the program, although again it bolsters me now and then to go over their credentials, their places and successes in the world, along with my own, to affirm my valuable citizen status when people and events conspire to make me feel even more marginal than I am proud to be--I see Nick brandishing up the road in his rocking seaman's swagger and sailing straight for my front porch. I knew the minute I saw him what he had come for. The only question was what was I going to do about it. And all I could think was, we are not talking about a man here who is my type or my age.

The wide open front door invited all of that fine Sunday that could ride in on the sweep of bright sunlight and high breeze of a glorious October day, and so many leaves had blown in that I was gathering them in my arms and remarking to the cat that we were going to have to rake the house. I scooped up an armful of the dancing brown oak leaves, straightened up and started for the door. At just that moment he rounded the bend in the sandy road and popped up on the scene like a dark puppet, the only figure in the back-lit forest landscape.

I walked onto the porch, threw the leaves over the railing and by way of greeting and defending sat on the step to watch his progress up the bumpy road.

He was alone, dressed in a clean shirt and jeans, Sunday best, with his best smile on. I recognized the smile; I'd seen it often enough during the past week when he would be hunkered down on a catwalk outside the window, dark-haired, patient and intent, painting the tiny lattice trim with an enormous brush in quick precise strokes, never missing, never hesitating, never looking down the twenty feet to the ground. He'd be hooknosed into it, concentrating, his dark eyes riveted to the yellow strokes. But when I walked by sometimes, his concentration would pop like a soap bubble and he'd look up with that smile as quick and sure as a paint stroke. And here it was today.

I smiled back and felt a rush. I knew by this immediate and uncharacteristic flash of panic that something had happened--that I'd accepted his perfectly balanced gesture of longing and aggression. And thinking about it later, I realized that when I'd accepted or turned down men before, I'd never really recognized the crucial moment. Rather than the one I'd assumed, say something in a conversation, it had been in fact a moment like this one, much earlier in the game, much deeper under the cultural layers, distant ancestor to the utterance 'yes' or 'no.'

If a smile is a mask, then the one I was looking at just then masked everything and therefore nothing--a lack of confidence and fear of rejection sat there in that smile like paired twins to a cocksure confidence and knowledge of acceptance. I smiled back like the confused watchdog that starts wagging its tail at the intruder and asked him why he was on foot and he said because Jeff fired him and I asked again why.

--We got up early cause the season opens today you know, scalloping, and I was going to come out here and work alone and he said no he wanted me to go with him to the point to get Buddy's jeep out of the sand and I said I didn't want to go because who knows how long we'll have weather like this and he was really mad so I went with him but when I got in the truck I slammed the door --bam!-- and he puffed up and said who needs you anyway you may as well just pack up and go. So I got my gear. And here I am.

--But he needs you. He can't scallop and finish the house.

--I know. That's why I wanted to finish it. He's fired me so many times I can't count 'em anyway. We've worked for each other since we were kids. Anyway I didn't want to leave the island until tomorrow because I've got these checks to cash. So I thought, it's a great day, who can I go see? And I thought you're just up here by yourself and you don't know anyone here and maybe you'd like some Sunday company.

170

The big smile. A fisherman, Nick had been plying his trade all week. He'd told me that his girlfriend had broken off with him, 'by telephone yet,' and that he'd been kind of down lately.

--She said 'Nick, I like you. I just like him better.' She's a nurse; she went back to her old boyfriend. I guess I just got caught in the middle of something. Still, it hurts.

He would call out when he and Jeff left after the sun was too low for them to paint any more that day, 'Have a nice evening,' when I knew he knew and he knew I knew he knew I wasn't going anywhere. He'd drop his work and come to help carry in bags whenever I returned from errands.

I liked him and liked to talk to him from the minute I walked out on the porch to see what color they were painting the trim. 'Hysterical yellow,' said Nick. 'No, dumbbell,' said Jeff, 'Historical yellow.' But we all laughed and agreed that Nick had it right.

He told me he was half Greek, half Iroquois, and that was why he did a lot of high work, because heights didn't bother him at all. 'I'm not afraid of anything,' he'd say. With that smile. Looking at it right now, I wasn't sure just what to do about him. I live like a nun here, I kept thinking.

--Where's your stuff? I asked.

--Down at Buddy's.

--The same Buddy with the jeep in the sand?

--No, that's another Buddy. And we laughed.

--So what do you just stay here by yourself?

--Uh-huh. I know a few people. But mostly I stay alone. Read, write, draw, walk around in the lanes back here. They're so beautiful and quiet and the pine needles are like a carpet--I never knew. I used to worry about Hansel and Gretel, but now I see that they had it easy.

--Down there in that pine grove the pine needles are so thick it's like a bed. When we were working around here in the summer and it was real hot, I'd go down there sometimes and just stretch out, it was so cool and nice.

--So. Do you want to call Buddy?

--Not really. Not yet. I don't think he'll be there yet anyway.

--Well, I was about to have some lunch. You want some hippie lunch? I've got brown rice and broccoli and I was going to fry some up and see what happens.

--That's the only thing I have in my apartment to cook with, in New Bedford, I mean. A wok. I'm pretty good with it. In fact, I'm a good cook.

--You want to cook?

--Not really.

Nick pulled himself up at the counter to watch me, his face bright with this expectant gee-it's-nice-to-be-here smile.

--You like the island then? You must. You're here.

--Oh, I'm fascinated by it. I like the way people here think they're another country and talk about *America over there.*

--I come here every summer and try to get a night job so I can hang around the beaches during the day. I'd like to stay here now for a couple of days on the beach.

--But you don't swim now do you?

--Oh, I don't swim ever. I don't even know how to swim. I just like to go down and lie around.

--They tell me real islanders frown on swimming.

--I dunno about that. But I know I can't swim. And I'm a fisherman.

--You ever go overboard?

--Nope.

--You ever see anybody go overboard?

--Yeah. He was just washed over like a paper cup. But we got him back.

And then Nick was off on his fisherman stories, doing a sort of Othello to my Desdemona. I was mesmerized.

--It was in the blizzard of '78. We had a really rough trip. The waves were just washing over us like we weren't there. We didn't know if we were going to make it. We got back all right, but the boat right in front us got caught. It went down, and all twelve guys were drowned. They lost everybody. It was a bum deal, too, because they were sort of the good guys. Most of them were married, two were engaged, and they had all these kids, and they were the ones that got it. We were sort of the bad guys; everyone on the crew is single. And nobody would miss us that much.

--Oh, our families, our moms and sisters and stuff, they'd miss us, they'd cry. But they wouldn't cry like *that*. Their boat just broke up like a crackerbox and it was gone. And everybody on it. That was the worst. It was my first trip out. I always figured if I made it through that my first time, I can make it through anything. I guess the worst I ever saw was a guy get his head cut off. By the wire that goes to the mainsail. Everybody knows not to stand up behind that, but he just stood up and bam. Just like that. You don't ever stand up behind the wire. That's rules.

(I actually interjected some *ohs* and *ahs* and *whats* in here but they are not of real interest while Nick just plunging in and on with his tales is. Of interest too is the fact that he kept me quiet for at least an hour.)

--Fishing's not dangerous if you know the rules. And I like it because if you know your work and you do it, you don't have to take nothin' from nobody. My grandpa was a fisherman--my dad never was--and he always said, 'If you know where you're going and you know how to get there and how to get back, you don't have to take nothin' from nobody.' My grandpa, he died in his sleep next to some bimbo he picked up at the bar that night. He was sixty-seven; what a way to go. He just went to sleep and that was it. He and grandma, they'd been split for a long time. Fishermen don't make such good husbands. When they're home, they're drunk and then they're gone ten days maybe two weeks or more. They come in after a good haul and they've got maybe two thousand dollars. And they get paid in the bars. There's bars in new Bedford where they go when they get in to wait for their checks. And the bar cashes the checks right there. And they're already drinking by then, so you can figure it out that the wives don't like much of anything about it and they try like crazy to get something out of the guys before it's all gone. They say fisherman's wives have to be half saints and half whores to put up with their husbands and keep them too. I know one guy, his wife always ·makes him bring her a gold chain every trip he has to bring her a gold chain when he comes home. She says it's so she will have something.

--And the guys who aren't married of course who's going to stop them and all these girls know when the boats come in and they're right there in the bars and ready for you and your money. They know how you're going to feel when you come in, poor bastard, after two weeks out.

--All fishermen are notorious liar, you know that. They even lie to each other. No, they especially lie to each other. They make the new guys go out and watch for the mail buoy. Well, there's no mail buoy. They always do it to the new guys. I remember when it was me and if you'd like to know how that makes you feel when you figure it out, let me tell you it's about two feet high, that's how. Nothing they like better than getting their hands on a new guy.

--There was this guy who came down one day in this big silver car in this three-piece and he's got this dolled up wife in the car waiting and he comes down to the boat and says he wants to get away from his life and his office and do something real. This completely cracked the guys up and it was so crazy I guess the captain thought why not and let him on the crew. He made it through the trip, which says something for him. He toughed it out even when he was sick which was most of the time. But he did these things you don't ever do on a boat. He shaved. No one shaved or even took baths on the old boats. He shaved. He used shaving lotion. We had to sleep in shifts in some bunks. And they put the new guy in mine. And he put talcum powder in it. Talcum powder.

-- I came off the shift and fell into my bag and that smell hit me and I jumped up and ran out and found him and I grabbed him and said, 'What the hell did you put in my bag?' And he said, 'I'm sorry, it just smelled so bad.' And I guess it did. But I was used to it, you know? I'd just fall in there dead tired and wrap it around me and all the familiar feeling, the smell was part of that, would be so comfortable like I knew where I was, you know? and I'd just drift off.

(I realize at this point that I have found, in Nick, the Proust of New Bedford.)

--I could've killed him. Gladly. He kept a diary which we of course read. With entries like, 'Well here I am out on the wide open sea under the giant endless sky.' and he would write about all us guys and say we were like animals and we'd sneak it out and read it and laugh our asses off. A humorist could've done something with that. But on the other hand, I don't know how it could have been any funnier than it was. We never saw the guy again. But if he did anything real with his life, I don't think it was as a fisherman.

After lunch, we drove to the beach through the beautiful gray-green island oaks that bent and reached over us in a dazzle of pale lights and shadows spangled with fall's first delicate red and gold. Nick said that once he had asked Carly Simon for a date and that she had been really nice about it, just said she was seeing someone else and thanks anyway and didn't treat him like a moron for which to this day he liked her and thought she had a lot of class.

Walking through the leaf-kicking forest path that magically gives way to the sandy beach path, we passed the gray slatted wood fence where people leave their best beat-up Reeboks and Topsiders and Bass sandals before going up to the beach. The local residents were out in full force judging by the number of shoes, and sure enough here they all were, the older folks looking like battered Burberrys ads (long before anyone would have dreamed of the nonsense of making Burberrys pink or white), and the young ones like tattered fifties preppies. They have a sort of natural corner on this look here on the island.

As they passed, accompanied by their Labradors and Setters, carrying out their trash and wine bottles, they greeted us as if we were their own. But I knew that Nick stood out among them. He looks like what he is, a man who works for a living. He could be one of the guys working construction in Crete. He could be what he is, a fisherman. His difference is that he is what is called just a man. No one says writerman or doctorman; it is physical work that gets 'man' into your title.

I thought about how this was the closest I'd ever been to a man like that and walking on the beach beside him thought I felt some elemental force not only from the sea. It made me glad to see him gesturing and shouting into the roar of the waves and the terrific wind with a generosity of spirit that made me feel a part of it and him.

He showed me where the ships from new Bedford go through Quick's Point. And the wind I wanted to name, to call a dictionary name like southeaster, could be called that, he guessed, 'but we just call this a blow.' Occasionally, he stopped to pick up something from the beach, a frayed piece of huge nylon rope, a plastic egg carton, and he'd shout, 'Fisherman's trash. Everything goes overboard. And the plastic,' he yelled, shaking an egg carton in the wind, 'lives to be a million.'

He ran backward ahead of me for a while shouting, 'Hey, hey! This is nice. You're fun to be with. You're fun to talk to. You're nice.' The wind was blowing his dark thick hair straight back so that his widow's peak showed and I could see how clear and fair his skin was and how much Iroquois was in his facial planes.

--Nice nose, I said. Very Roman. No, Greek.

--No, broken, he said. Big guy, Six four. Hit me with a beer bottle but I got him. They had to pull me off him. They're still talking about it. Or anyway I am. You cold?

--No. You?

--I am.

--Let's get you out of here.

--I'm o.k. Want to go up in the dunes?

--We can't go up in the dunes. They're endangered. It's verboten.

--Let's go up in the dunes.

--No, I said, the moral majority.

We sat by a big rock sheltered a little from the wind. Two dogs came to play. Nick threw sticks for them and they came bounding back elated while he shouted *'Don't shake, don't shake!'* as they came pouring like fur fountains on their triumphant romp back for an instant replay.

Nick looked at Naushon island across the way and said that he'd talked to the guy once about being caretaker for that rock over there. I like to be alone, he said, and so I thought it might be good.

The owners called for their dogs. But the sheepdog wouldn't leave until Nick did. And then the genteel, ineffectual owner said good naturedly it looked as if Nick had a friend. Nick smiled 'yeah,' but I could tell how glad he was to get rid of the dogs and get off the cold wind-spitting beach.

When we stopped at the corner where Lambert's Cove Road meets State Road I said should we go down and see if Buddy's there now and Nick said no let's not let's do that later.

Nick's mother had been killed by a car when she went on the first real vacation of her life, he told me. His father had recently remarried, to a much younger woman. So when, a few days later, on Halloween, I said we should go as we were, the odd couple, he said he didn't see anything odd about it. 'My dad has a younger woman. I have an older one. And I'm not sure we haven't got a better deal,' he said with that smile. 'We enjoy each other,' he said, kissing me lightly, 'and we have a lot in common. You're sweet and civilized, and I am rough and tough.'

I learned things from Nick, about lottery numbers, for instance that I think otherwise might have passed me by. Switching on the ten o'clock news one night for the lottery numbers, he cried out, 'That's grandma's number!'

Grandma's number? I was astounded. But he patiently explained that people who bet regularly have a lucky number, a combination they use almost every day, so that they're essentially waiting for their number to come up, that Jeff's number was for instance 1737 so that when he heard that number, he'd know Jeff had won.

He said that when they told him about his mother's death, they sent only one cop, 'the nice old guy who used to try to help us out when we were young punks running around with broken down shotguns in our coats. If they'd been coming for me, I knew they would've sent two or three of the young guys, the tough ones. But when I saw the old guy standing there alone, I knew there was something really wrong.'

--Nick! Jane said. Nick! Oh, Nicky is sweet. I like him. But you know he's a heroin addict don't you? An intravenous drug abuser who probably has given you AIDS. You know that don't you?

--I know he used to be a drug addict, I said scowling at her, thinking how she loved sensational scenarios.

--Nick is a bad one, said Fritz. The man does not know right from wrong.

I found this characterization mean-spirited and set to contemplating how not knowing right from wrong suggests a certain saintliness. Look at the moral majority. Besides, I'd rather hear Nick's fisherperson lies than Fritz's endless monologues on the history of film any day. Any day. And Nick was so much nicer to look at, too.

Nick and I were on a roll. He won sixty-nine dollars in the state lottery using my phone number instead of his regular combination and regarded me from then on with an awe my civilized virtues never did inspire. Altogether, I don't know when I've felt more appreciated. Every day for a week he'd start to go and find an excuse to stay on the island one more day. He'd call and say he was still here because he had to see a man about a horse and he'd go on like that until he'd say I really just wanted to see you and I'd say me too. And then his boat went out and while he was gone, I left.

When I showed up on the island the next year, Jane said excitedly that she had just seen him.

--Nick's here. Nick's on the island now.

--Oh Nick! Oh. Nick, I said. But I don't want to see him. I mean I do want to see him. I mean I...uh...
And I stammered around a while before arriving at it.
But I just don't know what we're supposed to do about one another, you know? We're so different.

--Yes. I know, she said flatly. He feels the same way about you.

...

Rattling around this magazine picture house in the woods where I am staying with a cat friend while her person is gone, I find myself completely lost. The sun is warm, and I sit in it amazed and pleased to be getting sunburned in New England in October. But the nice house dislikes me. It makes me nervous. Too much stuff, too much decor, too much designer art. The magazines make me crazy: get rich, wear these weird, hot clothes, meet a sexy New York executive for fireside evenings and tennis. I can't get my bearings. I turn on one of the four television sets and sit before it, defeated.

Returning to the sea, I find my favorite beach, a long serene, golden curve in all my memories today is looking meaner than a junkyard. The sand is dirty and violently ruptured from last week's hurricane winds. The seaweed is piled like slimy collapsed condos along the shoreline. It smells and not good. The sea, so dancing sweet in all my dreams, lies there like an endless asphalt shingle. Only the dunes retain their grace. So I concentrate on them. But how odd it feels to walk along the beach sort of humming and whistling and looking politely the other way, trying to ignore the sea.

I look in the house for a book to read and find one on dieting that tells me if I will forgive my family and friends their sins against me, I will be thin forever. I am amazed at the length of the list of people I am willing to forgive. Most of them I didn't even know I was mad at. I enjoy the chanting of forgiveness in my mind and drift off into a trance of forgiving incantations. I come to, hungry.

The book says to love yourself and get you whatever you most desire to eat, money no object. Treat yourself like company. I ask me what I really want and reply that I don't care. But then I think of scallops and go out to buy some.

--No, they are out of season, says the woman smiling behind the State Road Cronig's counter, unless you know a family in Edgartown who would like to give

181

you some. Their licenses started yesterday. The rest don't get theirs until November first.

Who would believe the politics of eating on this island? And just when I was going to be so loving to me. Usually I have to take what I can get. Paying all this attention to what I want makes me as nervous as those ads. This isn't living. This is self as idol, idol-worship. The heartless heart of the contemporary scene.

I pour some tea on my graying hair to see if that does anything for my spiritual slump. It does lift me a bit, not just because it makes my hair shine, but because I believe it is not done by the people in these magazines.

Even a phone call from a favorite friend fails to cheer me beyond the moment that it ends. It is only when I sit down with the poems Suzanne has written on Crete, that have arrived today, that I am freed. The poems are good, so good the static fades. The world of Crete comes in, the sea, the fishermen, the laughter and the music on the buses. And in the moment that I turn the page from one poem to the next, I realize that I am happy. I am found in Suzanne's poems.

...

J ane and I are having lunch. She is obsessed with selling the condo. I am obsessed with St. Augustine. And so we are a rococo variation on the theme of the ladies who lunch. We sound like Nobel physicists in the lab, purifying a strain of total miscommunication.

--So I put it in for $200,000. That's for New Yorkers. The ad says right there New Yorkers. With three exclamation points. Now that New York Air is coming here, the place is going to be crawling with New Yorkers. They have so much money $200,000 means nothing to them. Nothing. And the maintenance of only $200 a month. They won't believe. I don't believe it. I should ask more.

--You shouldn't ask more. You want to sell it, sell it. Don't ask more. Listen, Augustine is driving me insane. His trouble is the trouble with Christianity in general, this violent dualism, this obsession with good and evil, power and weakness. It's all so male, so God-the-father, like all these men of our generation they're so hung up on power, they don't know the world exists outside the little kingdoms of their influence. Augustine has it figured, though--confess and kill...

--Thirty minutes to New York, that's what will get them. I put that right in the ad, too. God. I can't go through another summer renting that place. It was like a cottage industry: put in the ad, wait for people to call, take them over--never mind what I was doing just drop everything and run over to show the place to some family with six kids and three dogs. And even when I got good ones, just a nice couple, you know, the things they did to the place. I can't tell you. It's too disgusting.

--Confessing to being human! It would be laughable if it didn't run so deep in the Judeo-Christian stream, which is to say our lives. But it is the real trouble, the deep trouble. Think of it, all this absurd breast-beating about being what you are. We are human. Who does Augustine think he is tearing his hair out because he stole a couple of pears from the neighbor's orchard when he was a kid, vilifying his willfulness, his having to do it because it wasn't to be done. Isn't that how we all grow up into the world, become ourselves, by resisting, questioning, trying things our way? What makes him think he is so fascinatingly evil?

--Who?

--Augustine.

--Oh, yeah him. Thank god I've got it rented through the summer this year at least. It was Jeff's idea, to put in the ad that rent could be applied to a down payment if the people decide to buy it. I never would have thought of that. Jeff has a knack for these things. I don't know what I'd do without him.

--Jeff is great. The condo's great. You'll sell it in a minute. But this male dominance in Christianity is so blatant, I don't see how women ever fell for it at all. I mean and still think of themselves as people. Maybe we don't. Look at Milton-- and I love Milton--he's got old Eve there just like she is in Genesis, created for the job of helping in the garden, serving balanced meals, and taking the rap for everything. Of course his Adam's whole trouble is with his own authority, which he, Adam, is insufficiently impressed with. The first thing you know, the whole thing gets out of hand and Adam is telling Raphael, the angel who's come for lunch, that Eve somehow seems wiser and better than he.
--Maybe $200,000 is too high. No. They wouldn't even want to look at anything for less. New Yorkers like to

spend a lot of money. They think if they do, they've got something.

--See, Adam's being uxorious--*what a word*--is the implied reason for the fall in Milton. Raphael warns him like some biblical popular psychologist to have more self-esteem, be more assertive. But Adam is so taken with Eve that he listens to her, eats the apple, gives up paradise so that he can be with her. So that of course means it is all her fault, our fault, we women. Milton is saying *this is how it happens, guys, you listen to these bitches for one minute and the next thing you know, you're in the labor force...*

--I do know this. If I don't sell that condo soon, I'm going to kill myself.

--Please don't do that. Why do women always turn on themselves? Oh, the misogyny of the whole Christian thing. Those old fathers, hiding behind Eve's skirts, saying 'We didn't do it Father, it was her. We don't know anything about it.' But of course Eve had no skirts.

--What in God's name are you babbling about? Are you nervous about something?

--Yes. Augustine. And Milton. And Stephen.

--How can you be nervous about Stephen? You've got all the cards in your hand.

--What if he's back there breaking up this twenty-year marriage, imagining that I'm going to come and sit at his feet by the fire for the next hundred years?

--Marriage? What marriage? They've been separated for three years. You're not breaking up anything. It was already washed up.

--It just makes me nervous, that's all.

--Look. You've got control of the situation. The man calls and says he can't think of anything but you for two weeks, you are in charge.

--But I don't want to be in charge.

--Who says you're going to break his heart anyway, if that's what you're so worried about?

--Do you know how many times I've been through this?

--You are really arrogant.

--I don't mean breaking hearts. I mean backing out. All the same, I don't like it. I don't want the blame. They blamed Eve for everything, though. It doesn't matter much what you do, you're going to get the blame. So I feel guilty. Just what they want, those God-the-father guys who have had us in their grip since the dawn of history. You know Copernicus was afraid to tell them that the earth revolved around the sun, that they weren't the center of the universe, because they would have burned him to a crisp.

--Helen. Shut up. You're driving me crazy. You've got nothing to worry about.

--I have the human condition to worry about.

--The...what human's condition? Be specific. You are crazy.

--Your condition. Mine. Ours. It makes a difference how we lead our lives.

--I don't know what you're talking about. Why don't you just make a decision about Stephen and shut up.

--Decisions. I don't like them. They're unnatural. Nothing growing, changing, becoming. That's not life. Life is disorderly and we do not control it. Why do you think they call it life?

--Oh, shut up.

--Well, you are crazy dear if you think that life can be ordered into this snap-down path made up of your decisions. The world the way you order it. The tiny world, the brittle, deadly world made of decisions.

--It works for me.

--It works and doesn't work.

--It works.

...

The tiny house is shining in its clearing in the winter night. I get out of the car and stand in the misted light of the full moon, ankle deep in a crisp carpet of frozen oak leaves. I have been gone for months and feel like I am home again.

The door opens without argument, verifying that I am no longer in Paris or New York but on the island, in the West Tisbury woods once again. Everything in the one-room house affirms the kind of innocence and natural charm found in the basic dream of the cabin in the woods.

Bob, my landlord, appears all rumpled in jeans and a navy sweater, the look of these parts--as though you've slept in your clothes for a week, or perhaps as though these are not clothes at all but the natural exterior of the natural man. Asked what the big news is on the island these days, he replies with a wry, regretful smile that at this time of the year, passing someone on the road can be the high point of the day. And I remember. Yes, I say, I started talking to myself in the car waiting for the ferry over. It all comes back so quickly. And we laugh the rueful laugh of people who know too well the look of shadows on the wall in the endless frozen solitary nights of a New England island winter spent alone. Bob says he and his wife spend a lot of time in Boston and will be going there on Wednesday. I have a tiny flash of panic, oh, alone!

But as I unpack and put things away, deciding how to actually live and work here, I feel myself relaxing into the serenity of solitude. It is the first time in a long time I have had a place of my own, and I am mindful, grateful that my life is centered now, and here.

The moonlight streams in the high glass triangle where the wall meets the gable of the roof. When I turn the inside lights off, I see by the porch light that it is snowing softly, drifting benediction, lovely, white, upon my house. I fall asleep looking at the moon, the drifting clouds, and the black arms of trees that reach across them.

Morning comes before I know I've slept, in a soft Wedgwood gray that hints at blue. In this half-glass house, natural light will set the rhythm of the day; I'll sleep with moonlight, starlight on my bed; I'll wake when the sun says it's time. I'll be a creature like the birds, a part of nature. A look around the place turns up no sign of fellow fauna. For now it's February and for now I'm it.

But other forms of life will come with Spring, and I'll be here to watch it all unfold.

And so I keep a watch for critters. The number of nature watchers on this island, and nature diaries, must be enormous. Everybody waking watchful, the journalists all poised with pens and cameras to scoop the first appearance of the squirrel and chickadee. The critters probably have stage fright; I can just see them huddled down south a ways saying to one another, 'No, you go first. I'm not going to be the first to show up there. I'd feel ridiculous.'

I'm not saying it's cold here, but when I wake early one March morning, I can see my breath, and when I open the refrigerator door, a rush of warm air meets me. By the tenth, it is 77° in Kansas City, and snow obscures the ground and branches here.

By mid March, we have black birds, chickadees and nuthatches. And in my house, a mouse Olympics; they swim across the water in the sink and race across the Havahart trap, skittering in a metallic frenzy for glory.

On April fourth, Bob and I bury the flicker who flew into my high broad window. I read Wallace Stevens' 'Waving Adieu, Adieu, Adieu,' over him, asking first if Bob thinks he'd rather have the poem about the eagle because it has the line 'Speak of the dazzling wings,' and the flicker might think it was about him, about the yellow in his wings.

Bob says no he doesn't think so because eagles prey on his kind.

As we kneel to push earth over the flicker, admiring his dazzling wings, his tiny flick of red like a touch of pathos for the fatal flaw of living, we look up to see between us tiny buds on the branches of a bush. Look. Spring.

On April fourteenth, the yellow finches come, female first; then two days later, two males. Then another female. A double date. On April twenty-second, the female cardinal comes, and on the twenty-fourth, the male. It's standing room only at the feeder by the twenty-fifth. Finches of every variety dive-bomb each other from the nearest tree, new arrivals trying to persuade the first sitting from holding the tables too long.

Finally one evening in late April, a tiny blue bird shows up on the ground beneath the feeder. He's disarmingly polite; while finches fly in circles of contention above him, he has his dinner, folds his napkin, and goes home. I wake the next morning at six, and there he is again. I begin to live for the Indigo Bunting, and every time he comes I am in ecstasy. And then one day he doesn't show up. I never see him again. I am abject. But am I not the one who believes in life's gifts as gift and not possession? I don't care what I believe. I want him to come back.

One May morning when Robin is visiting, she's walking past the Mill Pond and two of the red-rubber headed Muscovies are blocking the road, one in each of the two lanes. A woman in a car calls out to her.

--There are ducks in the road!

--I know, Robin calls back.

--Well, the woman shouts, do something. Aren't they yours?

Robin when she gets home wonders who this woman thinks she is.

--The Goose Girl?

...

190

Neil is sitting on an old green metal milk box from the Whiting Milk Company, near the edge of his football-field size garden. He is watching me plant beans. He leans intently forward on his cane, participating vicariously in the gardener's role as I bend along the turned-dirt rows, placing a bean seed every two inches, one-half inch into the soil, as instructed.

Famous, locally of course, for his own gardening, Neil has assigned this simplest of tasks to match my superlative inexperience in the garden. I've never planted anything. He picks the day and time he knows in his old bones to be the right ones for the beans.

--I never thought, he sings out, happy, I'd have a woman from Kansas helping me in this garden. And he shakes his head and laughs.

Kansas, another planet, it's the same to him. He's lived near Boston all his ninety years. I ask him if he's ever been out West and he says yes, he was sent out to Chicago for three years as a federal meat inspector. He came back from the war and took a job he kept until he retired. But Neil doesn't care much for travel. As he begins to understand my lifestyle, he says it takes all kinds I guess. And I say well, it takes two kinds, one to dig in and one to keep a look out.

When he retired to the Vineyard in 1960, he bought some land in Vineyard Haven for a cent a foot. He laughs and says he made a killing on it, though. 'I sold it a few years later for five cents a foot.'

The land we're planting beans on now is worth a scandalous amount of money. But Neil like all good long-time Vineyarders is not impressed except to think that people are crazy to be so greedy, to let things get so out of hand. He lives a simple, good life in his island home.

--This was a good place to retire, he says. I got what I wanted. Space.

In May, when his longtime neighbor, Ann, saw me preparing for flight from the island summer and its greedy rents, she took my part and sent me to talk to Neil about the tiny guest house behind his own house.

His wife had died only a few months before, and I found an old man with beautiful white hair sitting in his chair before the television. He had a very fixed rectangular jaw and great brown eyes made larger by thick glasses. His arms and chest were those of a powerfully built man. Everything about him seemed fixed, perhaps in part because arthritis kept him almost always in his chair. I tried to speak my name clearly, and then my business.

--Ann told me you might rent the little house to me this summer.

--No, he said, I won't rent it to you. But before my heart had time to sink, he added, I will give it to you if you'd like to stay.

And so it happens that I am in the garden at Neil's, planting beans. Neil sets about such projects as fixing the broken step at the guest house. When people say how nice it is that I'm taking such good care of Neil, the answer is that it is he who takes good care of me. He and I both love a laugh, so we sit around and talk a lot. He has a gift for storytelling, and a great sense of timing.

Two days after we've planted the beans, I hear him pushing the wheelbarrow past my window; then the rattle stops. Knowing him, I know he's up to something good. He calls out to me.

--Helen, your beans are up!

And I know right then that gardening is for me, if only I can last a growing season.

Epilogue

T hings change. The earth rolls over and the day is history. Almost everybody and everything in this narrative turned into a vanishing act. Charlie and Tina have sold Alley's and moved to North Carolina, their shining new license plate appropriately declaring them 'first in flight.' Diane is married now, and maybe she gets to cook enough at home because she no longer makes the daily soup at Alley's. Henry Beetle Hough is dead. Lambert is dead. The laundromat is gone, the wrong road sign, too. The library building is being abandoned for a building that would look right, as one summer visitor said when he looked at the rendering, with a 'Friendly's' sign over it. Things change. Things change. And not always for the better.

The hotel Saint André des Arts, last time I checked, costs five times what it did in 1984. Phillip and Neil no longer have their act together.

Phillip is a successful television model who spends his time flying first class between European capitals, being picked up by limousines and briefed on what product it is he's there to pitch. The good part is that sometimes he plays the piano a little in the middle of a spot.

Luis disappeared and although Phillip searched for him all over Portugal in perfectly adequate Portuguese, he did not find him. We assume he is with Isabelle and the beau-iful baby somewhere around Algarve. The baby *is* the most beautiful child any of us has ever seen.

Suzanne won an award of $100 a couple of years ago with which, she reported, she bought 'Jockey for Her' underwear, a Walkman, and a quart of Bombay gin. She comes to the island and swims straight out for an hour or jogs for ten miles, then comes back nonchalant. She has a PhD now and is the official poetry person at Boston College. She is on track.

Robin has a master's degree in international business management and a real job. Joel is still jammin', and may he ever jam. Dewi is at Yale.

Bonnie has gone rockabilly, having her childhood at last. Phillip tried to tell me.

--She has lacquered purple hair that juts straight out to *here,* he said.

--Oh, pshaw, I said, or something like it.

But I should have learned by now to believe Phillip. When we met her at the Relais Odéon for breakfast one Sunday last January, she had purple lacquered hair that juts out to *here.* She was wearing a red plaid micromini. And she was concomitantly only mildly interested in seeing me, for which I do not blame her. Things change.

About the only thing that remains constant as this narrative goes to press three years after the end of the span it covers is that Jane's condo is still for sale.

I am living in a real house now and working at the library, which confirms my prologue premise that the fates will guide or drag us to what we are, that is to what we love. The trick may be in knowing when to end the search, how to persist in loving what we've found.

I hope not to exasperate friends and family with this effort to record the vanishing acts that were our lives during the two years covered by this narrative. I've tried to speak true, that is, not to lie. But it is most likely that people who were there with me would say, *but it wasn't like that at all, not at all.* Maybe that's why people write novels, because it's all fiction anyway.

It seems odd to me, too, when I read this over sometimes, to be telling on myself in this way, as though volunteering a good clinical case record for the books of this brilliantly cheerful maladjustment. But I wanted to do it, in part as encouragement to other people--read especially *women*--to think of their lives as their odysseys, as their own, and in part because I loved these two years as though they were my own.